ONE MAN IN A VAN

A Roving Entrepreneur In Southern Spain

GEOFF CORLESS

Text copyright ©2017 Geoff Corless

The author has asserted his moral right under the Copyright, Designs and Patents Act, 1988, to be identified as the author of this work.

All rights reserved. No part of this publication may be reproduced, stored in a retrieval system, or transmitted, in any form or by any means, without the prior permission in writing of the publisher.

Introduction

Despite the similarity of the title, this book isn't a mere sequel to *Three Men in a Van*, the light-hearted and somewhat satirical account of the camper van trip which I planned and carried out with my friends Harry and Jeremy in the late spring of 2016. In that mildly humorous volume it has to be said that Jeremy was guilty of exaggerating our foibles – Harry's and mine – in order to spice up his story, common practice in the plethora of 'laugh out loud' travel books which amateur writers are wont to subject us to in this age of ever-shortening attention spans.

This book, by contrast, is a sincere attempt to recount the events that followed my return to Spain that summer; events of such intrinsic drama and suspense that any creative embellishments are rendered unnecessary. As our month-long trip laid the foundations for my subsequent activities in Andalucía a brief perusal of Jeremy's gallant attempt at authorship wouldn't go amiss, but the reader of that frivolous tome would be well advised to take his playful character portraits with a large pinch of salt, lest he or she begin the following work with an unduly derisive view of its author, who in point of fact resembles Jeremy's depiction of him very little, if at all.

This, therefore, is a stand-alone account of my singular attempt to carve out a career for myself in post-crisis Spain in which I have stuck to the facts in the manner of serious authors of old, as I am convinced that the intelligent reader demands and deserves far more than the current batch of scribblers can provide. Without more ado, I leave you with my earnest account of the most remarkable period in my already varied and action-packed life.

1

On the flight back from Gibraltar after our trip – having safely parked Bambi, my small but adequate camper van, on the Spanish side of the border – I immediately set to planning the tasks I would have to undertake in order to return within a week or so. My prospective employer, Hugo the Belgian, was keen for me to begin the job of revitalising his ailing enterprise, or enterprises, as I still wasn't altogether sure with whom I was dealing, or what exactly he dealt in, except imported luxury cars. While I pondered on the logistics of my rapid turnaround my two companions chatted idly, as they often did, about trivial matters. Although I had enjoyed our leisurely traversal of Spain from north to south I was eager to part company with my friends who, being recently retired, didn't share my ambition and vitality.

Harry, a stout, straight-talking ex-policeman, is a hearty fellow prone to unwarranted outbursts of wrath, though calmer of late due to having met a homely Belgian lady called Laura. Cupid's arrow had hit him right between his fleshy ribs and he was convinced that their brief encounter was destined to lead to a lifelong liaison, an assumption I was loath to douse with the cold water of common sense as, notwithstanding my extensive knowledge of the fickleness of womankind, I concluded that he had little to lose by throwing in his lonely lot with that pleasant and apparently wealthy lady whose chubbiness complemented his own considerable bulk. Besides, as Laura was a good friend of Hugo's it was in my interests to encourage their fledgling courtship in order to secure allies on Spanish soil, as when I finally cast off my employer's shackles and set up on my own – something I intended to do sooner rather than later, as a man must be his own master – it would be as well to have potential investors at hand.

Harry, therefore, had almost as much to think about as myself, as after showing Laura the wonders of North Lancashire he intended to join her in her fine house in the pretty village of Canillas de Albaida, just half an hour inland from Hugo's premises near the coastal town of Torre del Mar, a place slightly marred by foreign tourists, but still unsullied enough for my taste, me being a fluent Spanish speaker and confirmed Hispanophile ever since the marvellous years I spent in Jaén as a younger man, though I am by no means old now, having passed fifty not so very long ago.

Like me, Harry would have to vacate his flat, store his belongings and sell his vehicle – assuming he and Laura didn't fall out during her impending visit – while Jeremy would merely return to his patient wife June in Carnforth. There the bourgeois pair would enjoy their early retirement from the teaching profession and try to entertain themselves as best they could, in Jeremy's case by penning the book I mentioned earlier. I'm sure his idle scribbling helped to while away many a winter evening – his wife being very partial to prolonged and indiscriminate TV viewing – and I can only assume that his imagination got the better of him as he reinvented our trip to suit the whims of modern publishing, but I digress, as while he was tapping the keys and pretending to be Jerome K. Jerome I was already embroiled in mercantile manoeuvres of an audacity that a mere pedagogue could scarcely imagine.

"Well, it's been quite an experience," said Jeremy as we pulled up outside my apartment in Kendal, his wife June having been kind enough to drive me there after dropping Harry off at his seedy flat in Lancaster – a place which I had advised him not to show Laura lest she begin to doubt his solvency, to which he had responded in his usual brash fashion by telling me not to be so damn stupid.

"Yes, it's been a great trip," I said, conscious of the fact that a month of freedom was a novel and unlikely to be repeated experience for my generous, perceptive but unadventurous friend. "Thanks for the lift."

"So will you share a storage unit with Harry then?" he asked, pushing back the wavy grey hair that I believe he thought made him look rather intellectual.

"Oh, I don't know. I have so few belongings that I thought I'd take you up on that offer of a little garage space."

"And the Harley?" he asked.

"Well…"

"You can leave some stuff *or* the Harley, but not both," said June, having swivelled in her seat and fixed her beady eyes upon me.

I was about to respond when Jeremy adopted the conciliatory tone I'd heard so often during our trip when attempting to make Harry, and occasionally myself, see reason.

"Geoff, if you're really serious about going to live in Spain, I think you ought to sell the Harley now while it's still on the road."

"That bike is very precious to me. It's almost forty years old, you know."

"It sounds like it," said June with a titter.

"Well, let me know what you decide," Jeremy said, ignoring his wife's vain attempt at humour. "You can either ride the bike down or I'll come and pick you up with your stuff."

Realising that June's decision was irrevocable and that she undoubtedly ruled the roost, I said that I'd let him know soon.

"Good. You can soon pick up another motorbike in Spain when the money starts rolling in," he said as we stepped out of the car. He grasped my hand and gazed at me in a fatherly, or older-brotherly, way that he had, an expression no doubt cultivated during his decades of drudgery in the classroom. Who would have guessed that behind that benign countenance lurked a brain that would turn our mundane trip through Spain into a comedy, of sorts, at the expense of his best and oldest friends? There's nowt as queer as folk, as Harry might have said, but despite his libellous book Jeremy has always been the more obliging of the two and would prove to be a steadfast ally during my entrepreneurial odyssey, due perhaps to feelings of guilt regarding the scurrilous tale he was typing at the time, which I will mention no more, as nobody's perfect, not even Jeremy.

Alone in my apartment at last I opened the fridge to extract a can of beer, only to inundate the kitchen with water, the electricity having been cut off in my absence, an oversight that only spurred me on to vacate my home of three years as soon as possible. After shopping for food and candles I immediately began to pile up my belongings in the living room and was pleased to see that I'd accumulated remarkably little essential baggage, having always been a man who put experience and adventure before possessions. Unlike Jeremy and Harry, no one profession had ever satisfied me, and nor had one woman, as life is too short to spend it wallowing in domestic bliss when there are so many women to be loved and, inevitably, left. I could write a book about my amorous adventures and another about my varied professional career, but my publisher has requested a concise, no-holds-barred account of my Spanish endeavours and that is what they will get first, before we discuss more lucrative terms for any future works.

As I sipped the warm beer my thoughts turned to my beloved motorcycle which a neighbour grudgingly allowed me to park at the end of his private parking bay where there was space aplenty behind the little Smart car that he kept threatening to trade in. Carmela, my secret name for my Harley, was safe and sound in there, while poor Bambi was exposed to the elements and possible vandalism on the mean streets of La Línea de la Concepción, the town next to Gibraltar. Jeremy and Harry had never tired of poking fun at my trusty van, believing she would grind to a halt or explode before our journey's end, but I knew all along that my shrewd purchase would not buckle under the relentless punishment we subjected her to. As Hugo the Belgian had led me to believe that I'd soon be living in a deluxe apartment and driving luxury cars, I wasn't sure what Bambi's destiny would be, but as the electricity had been cut off – and the gas too, it turned out – I decided to return to Spain and retrieve her as soon as was humanly possible.

So it was that the very next day I kicked Carmela into life and rode her to Lake Windermere and back, before regretfully turning her custom handlebars and entering the forecourt of Kendal's best motorcycle dealership with a lump in my throat, a lump that became a boulder when the dastardly opportunist quoted me his price.

"£1800? You must be joking. This is a vintage Harley Davidson," I said, leaning nonchalantly on the seat to conceal a small tear.

"It's not that old, it's only a Sportster and it needs work," said the oily young scamp.

"What work?"

"A new exhaust for a start. Have you not heard the racket it's making?"

"It is a Harley, you know, not one of those effeminate Japanese bikes," I protested, though it was true that I'd been drawing more admiring stares than usual.

"It sounds like a pre-war tractor. Eighteen hundred's a fair price."

A glance at her balding tyres reminded me of another set of wheels I would have to dispose of.

"Listen, if I throw in a quality mountain bike, will you give me two grand?"

"We don't do pushbikes."

"No, but this one's a bargain," I said, before explaining that I had to sell off my bulky possessions within a couple of days due to having been offered a lucrative job in Spain.

He smiled and shrugged his shoulders, before saying that he might as well take a look at what I had to sell during his lunch break, so I gave him my address and roared off on Carmela. To cut a long story short, I eventually browbeat the callow youth into giving me two thousand for the Harley, the mountain bike, my old twelve-string guitar, a fish tank and a large reptile cage. So, while saddling the naïve youngster with those old things I also began to hone the bargaining skills which I would soon be putting into practice on Spanish soil. After calling Jeremy to tell him I had a mere bootful of treasured possessions to leave with him, including many photo albums in which the highs and lows of my extensive love life had been snapped for posterity, I popped over to the library to book a flight from Liverpool to Malaga, before calling him back to take him up on his kind offer of a lift.

"Tomorrow evening? That was quick," he said.

"Time waits for no man, not even me. I want to collect Bambi asap and get up to Hugo's to start work."

"OK, listen, why don't I pick you up tomorrow morning, then we can have lunch here before I drive you to the airport?"

"Sounds good," I said, not having eaten a cooked meal for a while.

"I'll invite Harry to lunch too. I'm sure he'll want to see you off."

"Fine, yes, that'll be nice."

That afternoon I called my landlord and requested the return of my £400 rental deposit, to which he replied that I had to give him a month's notice, not just ten days, and that he'd be coming round to inspect the place thoroughly in case four hundred wasn't enough to cover the damage. Rather than lowering myself by remonstrating with the seedy little man I hung up and decided against giving the place a thorough clean as I had intended. Having always been too much of a free spirit to ever buy a house, I had come to know the landlord class over the years and had reached the conclusion that no matter how hard you try, you can never please those grasping devils. Having rented five places in my native city of Lancaster and four more in Kendal, I had grown to loathe their grumbling ways, as whenever my dynamic life obliged me to move on there was always *something* about the vacant dwelling that displeased them. I'd had to point out that if the bed sagged due to vigorous lovemaking it was, in my book, normal wear and tear, and if the large lizard I once owned had damaged the carpet, or a Labrador puppy had chewed the curtains, furniture and skirting boards, surely that too should be factored into the rent? One old miser objected to me dismantling Carmela in the kitchen of a ground-floor flat, while another grouched about my mellifluous guitar playing disturbing the neighbours, so by this time I was resigned to their devious ploys, and besides, my work for Hugo promised to be so lucrative that I soon hoped to purchase my very own country pad, house prices being pleasingly low in Spain at the time.

***

When Jeremy arrived the following morning I had cleared away the candle stubs, but done nothing more to beautify the place. As it wasn't the first time he had assisted me in this way, a silent grimace was his only response to the cobwebs and general griminess that had accumulated during our month in Spain and we were soon trundling down the motorway en route to his detached house on the outskirts of Carnforth. As we entered the long driveway to the Edwardian dwelling I chuckled to myself as I reflected that it had taken Jeremy and June a lifetime of toil to eventually possess that fine house, while within two years I expected to take ownership of a large chalet with a swimming pool – one of those infinity pools if possible – as Hugo the Belgian had spoken in no uncertain terms about the vast amounts of money to be earned by importing cars and carrying out other transactions that he had promised to fill me in on in due course.

After we had stashed my stuff in the boxes in the garage that June had allotted for the purpose, Harry arrived in his scruffy car and we all sat down to a paella that June had made in honour of my swift, and Harry's slower, departure for Spain. Working full-time in the classroom for almost forty years meant that she has never really honed her culinary skills, but I managed to get it down with the help of two glasses of 1982 Rioja which Jeremy had brought up from his small wine cellar, also in my honour.

"Here's to your new adventure, Geoff," said our host, before we all clinked glasses.

"You haven't wasted any time," said Harry, while June filled his plate with another helping of gooey rice.

"Well, you know me, always keen to strike while the iron's hot. I just hope Bambi hasn't been stolen."

"I doubt it. Decorated maybe, but not stolen," he said. "Still, you only need her to get you back to Torre del Mar, then you'll have better things to drive, eh?"

"Yes," I said, wincing at the thought of a graffitied Bambi, because for all her shortcomings she was effectively a home on wheels which I might have to sleep in for a few days, I thought then. "When do you think you'll be heading to Spain?"

"Oh, Laura's coming next week, for ten days, so I reckon about a month from now, once I've put my stuff in storage and sold the car. Oh, did you get shut of the Harley?"

"Yes," I said. Having told Jeremy on the drive down how much I'd been given for the motorbike and other odds and ends, he had strongly advised me not to reveal the amount to Harry, as he considered it a very modest sum for all those items and he didn't want the laughing policeman to take the mickey out of me on our last day together until at least September, when they planned to come out to visit.

"How much?" Harry asked, rubbing his greasy finger and thumb together and gazing at me over the paella dish.

"Three grand," I said.

"Hmm, not bad, not bad at all, considering the state it was in. So you can add that to the little pile your aunt left you," he said, referring to a modest inheritance I had received some months earlier and whose true value I may have exaggerated in the heat of the moment, as my purchase of Bambi and subsequent expenses had reduced my capital considerably.

"Yes, I'll set that aside for when I decide to branch out on my own," I said, relieved that my little fib hadn't been detected by that would-be sleuth. I don't make a habit of lying, I swear, but if you knew Harry as I do you'd forgive that tiny white one, as he's just about the only person on earth who can wind me up, and the last thing I wanted was to retaliate with my own biting wit, as I wished to keep him sweet because one never knows when one might need a friend nearby, especially one living in a nice house with a pool.

"Oh, that reminds me. Don't you still owe Jeremy for the boat ticket?" said June with her usual disregard for mealtime etiquette.

"Yes, I'm going to settle up later," I said, smiling sweetly and patting my pocket.

After Jeremy had made the coffee June busied herself in the kitchen while my two friends began to reminisce about our recent trip as if it had been the event of a lifetime, which I suppose it was for them, but although I laughed politely at their quips my mind was already on more important things.

"You're flying this time, so at least you won't get seasick again," said Harry with a goofy grin, no doubt referring to my migraine on the ferry and my hangover in the kayak, but I just nodded and sipped my coffee rather than retaliating by reminding him of his abduction by the English-hungry campers in Burgos or his cowardly reaction to a piddling nuclear power station in Valencia.

"And make sure you don't get sunburnt again," the pedantic oaf added, nudging Jeremy, who smiled as serenely as me, being above such infantile gibes.

"Call me when you get to Laura's house. I'll keep my English mobile for now," I responded with a placid smile.

"I will, and I'll expect to see you roaring up that mountain road in a red Ferrari."

I chuckled indulgently. "Probably a BMW or a Merc, actually, as that's what Spanish buyers tend to go for." I turned to Jeremy. "We'd better make a move, I suppose."

"Yes, let's beat the rush-hour traffic."

June appeared just then and planted a kiss on my cheek and wished me good luck, before patting me below the belt, surprisingly near to my private parts. Though I was well accustomed to such handling I was astonished to receive such an intimate prod from my friend's wife, right under his nose, but when she mouthed the words 'boat ticket' I realised that it was the wad of notes she was interested in, so I duly whipped it out and peeled off twenties until Jeremy said 'basta' (enough), one of the few Spanish words he had picked up on our trip.

After telling her long-suffering spouse that he would have to scrape off the mess she had created in the paella pan she withdrew once more, so the three of us stepped outside and prepared to depart. While transferring my well-travelled bags from the back seat to the boot I spotted a photo album that I'd failed to retrieve, but before I could lay my hands on it Harry had whisked it away and begun to flick through my intimate graphic memoir.

"Bloody hell. Who the hell's this?"

To my intense annoyance – and I was already pretty annoyed by his cheek – the album wasn't the one of the divine Carmela (Jaén), the scrumptious Sarah (Garstang), the athletic Olga (Lancaster/Grimsby), or of several other passably attractive former lovers, but of Freya, the gruesome Swedish chambermaid. I cursed my luck and looked up at the sky, before attempting to snatch the revealing tome from his spade-like hands, but he's far faster than he looks and was soon around the car, gawping at my artistic photography.

"Who *is* it?"

"Freya."

"Bloody hell! That Denise you knocked about with was rough, but this one's something else. No wonder you never let us meet her. Look at this Jeremy."

"No thanks," he said sternly. "Give it back, Harry."

After one last goggle he handed it to Jeremy, who blanched a little while closing the book, before passing it to me.

"What do you think, Jeremy?" the blasted baboon cried.

"I didn't look."

"Yes, you did." He turned his gorilla-like body to face me. "No offence, Geoff, but I've never seen such an ugly woman in my life. What's up with her teeth?"

"She had two gold ones."

"Yes, like that Jaws fella in the James Bond film. She could be his sister if she weren't so fat."

Not much fatter than your Laura, I thought of saying, but I'm far too gentlemanly, and cunning, to stoop so low. I cleared my throat. "She insisted I take the photos after seeing some of my other albums. What could I do? Poor girl, she was lonely in Ambleside and needed cheering up. It was only a fling anyway."

"Well I'd fling that album away if I were you," said Harry weakly, somewhat quashed by my self-possessed response and Jeremy's reproving glare. It has to be said – as Jeremy says so often in his somewhat repetitive book – that he is a great mediator and peacemaker when the three of us are together, and once again his firm intervention had prevented a full-scale conflict, something that had never happened in our fifteen years of friendship, though on more than one occasion I had come close to putting my karate skills into practice to silence the great brute. I sincerely hoped that Laura's experience in the Belgian diplomatic service would stand her in good stead when we eventually met up, as if I were I to drive up to the village in anything less than a large German saloon car he would be hooting with derision in an instant.

"I hope Laura enjoys her stay here," I said, idly patting the album, as his Belgian matron is far from being an oil painting herself.

"Yes, where will you take her?" Jeremy asked.

"Oh, up the Lakes to a nice hotel, I guess," he said, now on the defensive lest I savage him with my biting wit, but Geoff Corless is a man who knows on which side his bread might be buttered, and he was conscious that he had two Belgian slices – Hugo and Laura – who he'd be well-advised to handle with care.

"Well, give her my regards and tell her I'm looking forward to seeing you both soon," I said, casually flipping the album into the boot, to be disposed of at the airport, as although Freya was a good sort and did remarkable things with her feet, she didn't quite deserve to enter my amorous hall of fame.

I have included this trivial anecdote not only to illustrate the childish and mean-spirited behaviour that Harry is capable of, but also to reassure my readers that I am not averse to criticism and am perfectly capable of disclosing my own shortcomings, which ought to convince you of the veracity of the rest of this extraordinary account, and that my slight inaccuracy regarding the motorbike money was an uncharacteristic though wholly justifiable fib.

Having assured you of my integrity, let us now make haste to Spain, where my adventure truly begins.

2

After giving The Rock no more than a cursory glance I marched over the border and past a park, eerie in the moonlight, before turning off towards the area where I had parked my Bedford Bambi mini-motorhome whose milky-white exterior belied her twenty-seven years. Having omitted to make a note of the street, so clear was its location in daylight, I toured around the southern side of La Línea for quite a while before I found her, safe and sound on a secluded side street. After pumping some air into her flaccid tyres, for I am a meticulous mechanic, I started her up, before concluding that I could do worse than spend the night right there. In a jiffy I was stretched out on one of her two slim beds and after luxuriating in my solitude for a while – a sublime joy after spending so many nights sharing the space and air with one or both of my erstwhile companions – I fell asleep fully dressed, so weary was I after my two-hour tramp around the dreary, sprawling town.

I had hit the sack at approximately 4.00am, so I awoke late and in a very sweaty state. Having omitted to open a window the temperature inside had reached forty-one degrees by midday, something I'd be as well to bear in mind if I were to spend a few more nights in there, although I was sure that Hugo would get me fixed up with a place pronto; either that or invite me to stay at his plush chalet until I located a small but stylish apartment not too far from the sea. Bambi's tardis-like interior doesn't stretch to a shower, so I settled for a quick wash at the sink before donning a clean t-shirt and scuttling over to the nearest bar. There I tactfully ordered my breakfast of coffee and croissants before making a beeline for the bathroom, as on the previous trip we'd found it expedient to avoid using the chemical toilet except in cases of dire emergency, due to it being an old and not entirely hermetic one, but fear not, for there will be no toilet humour in *this* book.

So, relieved, nourished and hydrated, I strolled back to Bambi and soon had her 1000cc engine purring like a kitten as I threaded my way out of that labyrinthine conurbation. With only myself on board she moved with far greater zest than when burdened with the colossal Harry and the normal-sized Jeremy, and I almost whooped for joy on finding myself able to match the speed of the traffic along the main road, so when I reached the toll road which would take me all the way to Torre del Mar – there being no viable free alternative – I slipped into the slipstream of a lorry carrying large lumps of marble and was thus able to fly along at eighty (k.p.h.) and avoid the toots of derision we had so often suffered when fully laden. I was ever so glad about this because on holiday one feels carefree enough to assimilate the jests, and occasional fury, of passing, or queueing, motorists, but as I was now a man about to embark upon yet another new career I was in no mood for such nonsense.

I was so serious about the venture which I felt sure would at last exploit my true potential that during the drive I kept my eyes on the lorry while my mind concentrated on the task at hand. I have a zen-like ability to shut out all superfluous thoughts and zone in on one subject, which in this case was creating a favourable impression on my employer, Hugo the Belgian, who I had met only once. Our interview had been relatively short and exceedingly positive, but here I was, about three weeks earlier than he expected and raring to go, but also eager to pin him down regarding my remuneration. He had mentioned generous commissions and also hinted at a basic wage, and although I'd told my friends that he'd promised pay me at least a thousand euros a month, this had been based on my own estimate rather than his actual words. I had named that figure, not to deceive them, but to avoid listening to hours of cautionary advice from the finicky Jeremy and the cynical Harry, both of whom had settled for a safe salary during their whole working lives and possessed none of the dash and bravado necessary to get ahead in the cut-throat world of commerce.

So engrossed was I that I inadvertently followed the marble lorry off the motorway and had travelled about twenty kilometres northwards towards Cordoba before realising my mistake, upon which I chuckled at my Einstein-like absorption and set about rectifying matters. Less than four hours after setting off I arrived in Torre del Mar, having slipstreamed a car transporter for the remainder of the journey and thus saved enough petrol to offset the cost of the tolls, I reckoned, though the driver had shaken his fist in farewell on realising that I'd been tucked so close behind him, sleek aerodynamics not being one of Bambi's salient features.

Keen to make an excellent second-impression on Hugo the Belgian, I located the lane to his country residence and pulled over to set about sprucing myself up. After shaving and applying deodorant to my potentially odorous zones I stepped into my suit, an M&S charcoal check wool number in which I looked slick but felt rather warm, before carefully knotting my Old Harrovian tie and combing my short, slightly greying hair. I looked rather distinguished in the wing mirror, but there wasn't a moment to lose as at 5.30pm the sun was still burning down and I would be well advised to vacate Bambi *tout suite* and get inside Hugo's air conditioned house.

On reaching the imposing lime-green chalet I drove through the open gates and parked beside a dusty Renault Twingo, Hugo's 'wheels' being presumably parked in the huge garage to the left of the two-storey house. On my previous visit less than a fortnight earlier a very different scene had greeted my eyes and ears when I had driven Laura's mini into the compound. Several smart cars had been stationed in the carport and much cavorting could be heard from the swimming pool located behind the house; not the strident shrieks of delighted children, but latino pop music, sundry splashes and fragments of lively adult conversation. On hearing several female voices I'd been eager to be introduced to Hugo's frolicsome ménage, but in the event our half-hour interview had taken place in a small, austere study situated at the front of the house, after which he had shown me to the car, pumped my hand and waved me through the gates, before – I saw through the wing mirror – scuttling off to join his playmates.

Now the place was silent and as I shaded my eyes from the slowly sinking sun my intuition told me that all was not well, a hunch shortly to be confirmed by the lack of response to my initially short and later prolonged ringing of the doorbell. The position of the porch was such that no shade was available at that hour and I began to sweat profusely in my suit. After loosening my tie a fraction of an inch, for I am not a man who loses his cool easily, I rang the bell again, before realising that the merry peals I had heard on my first visit were conspicuously absent. Undeterred, I rapped lightly on the solid door and listened intently for footsteps, before a trickle of liquid coursing down my spine told me that were I to stay there much longer I would become soaked from head to foot. I knocked louder, then louder still, until my slight irritation caused me to take off one of my brown suede brogues and hammer on the door with the heel, producing a din that couldn't fail to be heard from every corner of that ample residence. Sure enough, after drawing back my arm for one final onslaught, the door opened swiftly and I almost clobbered a slender young lady on the head.

"Qué cojones crees que estás hacienda, imbécil?!" she shrieked, which translates roughly as, 'What on earth do you think you're doing, foolish one?'

Wiping the sweat from my eyes as she lowered her arms, I beheld a face of such beauty that I staggered back and had to grasp a pillar in order to prevent myself from falling down the steps. Her gorgeous brown eyes bored into my not unattractive blue ones and as she took a step towards me I attempted to rid my head of its excessive moisture by running my hands over it, but the bristly nature of my hair caused a sprinkling shower to head in the direction of her looming, passionate face.

"Me cago en la leche! Qué guarro eres!" she exclaimed, meaning, 'Oh heck! What a piggy you are!' but as it would be pedantic to duplicate her every word I'll translate our subsequent conversation simultaneously.

"Geoff Corless, at your service," I said in my flawless Andaluz accent, before placing my right hand on my sodden chest and giving her a brief but solemn bow.

Having recovered from the initial shock of seeing a sartorially impeccable man hammering on the door with a shoe, or trying to, she flicked back her head of lovely dark hair and her divine face broke into a charming smile, her full lips revealing her flawless teeth, ever so white compared to her smooth olive-brown skin.

"You don't look like one of them," she said with a refined titter, and as one of them doesn't mean 'one of them' in Spanish I raised my eyebrows in an amused, quizzical way.

"Like who, dear?" I asked with a sweet smile of my own as I slid my shoe back on.

"Never mind. What do you want?" she purred, her husky voice complementing her feline figure.

"I have an appointment with Sr... Hugo. We have urgent business matters to discuss, er...?"

Coyly ignoring my request for her name, she sighed and scratched her cute little nose, before her now placid eyes opened in amazement. I checked that my tie hadn't slipped too much, but it was over my shoulder that she was staring.

"What in heaven's name is that?" she asked, a svelte finger pointing in the direction of Bambi.

"That... that is a small camper van which I have driven from Gibraltar... for a friend," I said, as although Bambi is a practical and in some ways attractive vehicle, one wouldn't normally attend a business meeting in her.

"It looks like a toy, an old toy," she said, stern again, maybe feeling that she ought to suppress her good humour in case I took her for a floozy, as there was no doubt in my mind that a certain chemistry was bubbling up between us. She was dressed in a tight black top which revealed her pert bosom and slim waist to perfection, and though her grey tracksuit bottoms were on the baggy side I had no doubt that they concealed a stunning pair of legs with wonderfully slim ankles, judging by her slender arms, delicate wrists and violinist's hands.

"My friend is a petite lady... from Paris," I quipped, raising my eyebrows to denote that I wasn't fibbing, but merely joshing her.

"A gypsy?" she asked, artfully concealing her amusement.

"Ha ha, no, not a gypsy," I said, flashing my gnashers and winking. "So, do you think Hugo will be able to see me?"

"Hugo is unavailable."

"Not in?"

"Unavailable."

"Right." During this period of sizing each other up I hadn't ceased to sweat, but had become unaware of it as I strove to achieve that all-important first impression which is so crucial with the ladies. Her pouring cold water on my hopes of seeing my future employer made me once more aware of the flow of warm liquid which was threatening to reduce me to a dehydrated wreck, so, setting aside our mild flirtation for the moment, I decided to ascertain exactly how unavailable the elusive old Belgian was.

"When will I be able to see Hugo?"

"I cannot say. I'm looking after the house in his absence."

"Can I come in for a moment?"

"No, I'm not allowed to let anybody inside."

"Are you his secretary?"

"Something like that. You must go now, as I have to lock the gate."

Unwilling to leave without discovering more about Hugo's mysterious movements, I decided to try to soften her up a little. Gazing at her serenely I slowly slid off my tie, rolled it up, and thrust it into a pocket, before taking off my now weighty jacket and draping it over the white balustrade. She feigned a look of boredom, but when I swiftly unbuttoned my peach-coloured shirt and peeled – and I mean peeled – it off I had her full attention once more. The shedding of the suit and revelation of my slim but tanned and muscular body must have taken twenty years off me in her eyes, and as I slowly wiped away the moisture with my shirt she looked on, open-mouthed.

"That's better," I said, tossing the sopping shirt onto the jacket and leaning on the balustrade. With my arms folded I was able to accentuate my ample biceps, by pushing them out with the backs of my hands, and as I rocked to and fro I looked into her eyes and waited for her to make the next move.

"Be careful, you're going to…" were her next words, but I didn't catch the rest, as I had leaned too far and fallen backwards, mercifully landing on a flowerbed. In an instant I perceived the mature rosebushes on either side of me, either one of which would have torn me to shreds or even impaled me, so I set about improvising my way out of this potentially embarrassing situation. Just as her startled face appeared above me I sprang to my feet, leapt onto the gravel and executed a few karate moves, before trotting up the three steps and resuming my position on the balustrade.

"Sorry, I hope I didn't scare you," I said with a chuckle as I casually wiped the earth from my arms, body and legs, striving all the while to control my breathing; no mean feat, I assure you.

"Are you hurt?" she asked anxiously.

"Of course not. I just did it to get your attention. Now, are you going to tell me when I can see Hugo, or not?" I said, pressing down on the balustrade to accentuate my glistening pectoral muscles.

"I cannot," she said, a smile of relief appearing on her pretty lips. "You must go now. Do you have food in that van?"

"No," I said, having forgotten about Harry's stash of cans under the bed.

"You look hungry. Wait here and I'll get you something."

"No, no, I'm not hungry in the least," I said, aware that some people confuse a lean, toned body with a thin one. "I would appreciate a drink though," I added, keen to buy myself time.

"Around the corner you will find some chairs. Wait for me there," she said, before stepping inside and softly closing the door.

I grabbed my clothes and rounded the corner of the house, where I found three wicker chairs and a table in the shade. Despite the fact that my woollen trousers were clinging to my legs, it was an immense relief to slump down and take the weight off my burning feet, and while I was waiting I realised that I had to convince the still nameless girl of my bona fide business credentials. When she arrived with a large bottle of cold water and a single glass I asked her bluntly who the 'them' were when she had declared that I didn't resemble one of them, or words to that effect.

"Who?"

"Them."

"Who are they?"

"That's what I'm asking you," I said, before rephrasing my question.

"Oh, them. Well, people who want to see Hugo as a matter of urgency."

"In that case I *am* one of them, because I certainly want to see him," I said with a chuckle, before downing a third glass of water.

"No, none of them are anything like you. They are always very serious and... forbidding. They want to see him, but he doesn't wish to see them, which is why he isn't here."

"That settles it, because he most certainly *does* want to see me," I said, before outlining our recent interview. As she still looked sceptical I then described the sounds I'd heard from the swimming pool. "Were you here that day, er?"

"Claudia. Call me Claudia."

"Geoff."

"I know," she said, still standing. "You were certainly very thirsty," she added on observing my rapid consumption of the water.

"Yes. Were you there that day? It sounded like there were a lot of people living it up."

"Yes, all was well then. Look... Geoff, you'll have to go now as I really must lock the gate."

"Can I call you tomorrow?"

"No, there are no phones here. Hugo insisted on no phones and to disconnect the intercom. It was stupid of me to forget to lock the gate."

I gave her an especially piercing stare, or rather gaze, as I intended to penetrate her now frosty façade and establish what lay behind those delectable orbs.

"But if you'd locked the gate you might never have met me," I said, raising my eyebrows, pouting slightly and nodding slowly, before rather spoiling the effect by attempting to pour water from the empty bottle.

"Ha, that's true," she replied, hiding her feelings admirably.

"Shall I come back tomorrow, dressed more... er, appropriately? We could swim together."

Her nervousness produced an involuntary titter. "The pool is empty and the furniture stored, in case of drones. Look, all you can do is come back, maybe a fortnight from now, and see if there are more cars. That will mean he has returned."

"Oh, come come, Claudia, dear. Why spend so long languishing here when we could be getting to know each other?" I said, valiantly resisting an almost insatiable urge to scratch my damp and itchy nether regions.

She shook her head in confusion and I knew she was tempted. The flesh is weak, after all, and if I could only come up with something to reassure her of my good intentions I foresaw a frolicsome fortnight ahead of me while I waited for Hugo to return. She must have been thinking along the same lines, as when I suggested fetching my guitar from Bambi she asked me how I had got to know Hugo.

"A Belgian friend of his arranged our meeting," I said.

Her face froze and her bottom lip began to quiver. "N-not Axel?" she asked, before covering her mouth.

"No. Who's Axel?"

"A monstrous man who is responsible for our present... never mind."

"No, it wasn't him. It was a sweet little lady called Laura."

"Laura?"

"Yes, Laura."

"Laura who lives in Cómpeta?"

"No, in Canillas de Albaida, not far from there," I said, as I have a photographic memory for maps, among other things.

"Ah yes, Canillas. Well why didn't you say so?" she asked, looking like a ten ton burden had been removed from her slender shoulders. She flopped down into a chair and expelled sweet air from her lungs, before pulling a packet from her pocket and lighting up.

"It didn't occur to me that Laura was such a significant personage," I said, declining her offer of a fag, as one doesn't look so much younger than one's years by succumbing to common vices.

"Oh, no, no, she's just a friend of Hugo's, that's all. Do you want a drink?"

"I've just had one."

"No, I mean a proper drink."

"What have you got?"

"Everything."

"In that case, a malt whisky would be nice, and another large bottle of water," I said, as I must have lost litres of liquid while standing in the sun. "Do you mind if I go and change into something more comfortable, Claudia?"

"Feel free. Oh, I'll come and lock the gate, but you must leave later."

"Of course," I said, though I was sure that after a friendly tipple she would change her tune.

After quickly washing my sweatiest zones in the van I slipped into a pair of shorts, a gym vest and sandals, before strolling back to the veranda where I found Claudia emerging with a tray of drinks. I politely ushered her ahead in order to observe her buoyant buttocks through her baggy leggings.

"Why don't you slip into something more comfortable?" I said as she leant over to lay down the tray.

"I'm fine. Sit down and help yourself."

I eased myself into a chair and crossed my tanned legs, being in no hurry to broach the new bottle of Glenfiddich. She looked at me in a perplexed sort of way, before mixing herself a gin and tonic, so I poured an inch of whisky into another glass and topped it up with water.

"Ice?"

"Good heavens, no, not with malt," I said with a gracious chuckle.

"Sorry to be a bore, but could you tell me how you met Laura?"

I explained the fortuitous circumstances of our meeting on the east coast of Almería, the friendship Laura had struck up with my portly friend Harry, and our short visit to her house in the hills.

"Hmm, sounds plausible enough. Does Harry or the other man know Hugo?"

"No, no, they were mere trippers. It was I who requested the meeting when Laura told me about his activities."

Her brow creased and her eyes narrowed in a most becoming way. She sipped her drink and looked at the sea, just discernible between two more large houses.

"Did she tell you about the car business?"

"Yes, that's right."

She turned to face me. "And nothing more?"

"No, though in our meeting Hugo intimated that there were other sidelines which he might wish me to become involved in," I said, keeping my cards close to my chest, though it has to be said that they were rather fuzzy ones.

Claudia slowly expelled smoke through her nostrils and sat back in the chair, looking truly relaxed for the first time since we'd met. I was about to edge my own chair a little closer, feeling that the time would soon be ripe for a little handholding, when she sat up straight again with a fervent gleam in her eyes. I thought, nay hoped, that she was about to whisk me off to her bedroom, as in my experience some women prefer to dispense with the usual preliminaries, but after taking a long drink she declared that she was going to telephone Hugo.

"But there's no phone."

"Of course there is, though the landline is disconnected. I can only call him on matters of urgency and your arrival may be a stroke of luck for him. He might be angry with me for calling, but I rather think he won't. Excuse me a moment, please," she said, before leaping lithely to her feet and striding away.

Intrigued by her snap decision I rose and crept to the corner, from where I saw her pause to look at Bambi, before stepping into the house and closing the door behind her. In a way it was rather frustrating that just when closer intimacy had seemed imminent Claudia had decided that business must come first. As I resumed my seat and poured myself another drop of whisky I reminded myself that I wasn't in Torre del Mar merely to add yet another notch to my metaphorical headboard, but to make the fortune that had so far eluded me. Claudia was ripe for the picking and when we became lovers I would have greater access to the Belgian kingpin, but it would be unwise to give the impression that my principle aim was to get my leg over. I moved my chair even further away from hers and patiently awaited her return.

Some twenty minutes later I heard her soft tread and assumed an expression of relaxed but alert pensiveness.

"Ah, there you are, dear. I take it you managed to speak to our boss."

"What? Oh, yes."

"And how is he?"

"Fine. You certainly like that whisky."

I smiled and nodded. "Merely rehydrating myself after my suspicious sweetheart forced me to stand in the sun for so long."

"What? Oh… ha, yes. You do have a funny way of expressing yourself, Geoff. Where are you from?"

"Merry England, though I spent many years in Andalucía; Jaén to be exact."

"What did you do there?"

"Teach. I'm a qualified teacher," I said, as I'd done a short correspondence course before securing the job.

"And what else have you done?"

"Oh, Claudia, do you have all night?"

"Er, no, you'll have to leave before it goes dark."

"Then I shall be brief," I said, before resuming my extensive curriculum, including my two years as an accountant, three years as an employment adviser and four years as a hotel manager, that final word just slipping out, as it was clear that she'd been asked to grill me regarding my past achievements, something Hugo had failed to do during our brief and upbeat meeting. In the interest of brevity I omitted a lot of less relevant jobs and she seemed satisfied with my response.

"Could you mix me another drink, Geoff?"

"Coming up," I said, before skilfully scooping out the larger ice cubes and mixing a G&T, including the lemon, at lightning speed.

"Thanks. Have you worked in a bar too?"

"Oh, I sometimes helped out my subordinates at the hotel," I said, though I've actually worked in two pubs, a cocktail bar and a crown green bowling club.

"I see." She sipped. "That's good. Do you have a criminal record?"

"Of course not."

"Not here or in England?"

"No." I smiled slyly. "Ought I to have?"

"No, it's important to Hugo that you haven't."

"Ah, he likes his men to be squeaky clean, eh? And his women, of course."

"Well... yes, that's it, but for the role you might have to play it's especially important that the filth have nothing on you."

She didn't say 'the filth' of course, as she was speaking Spanish, but *la pasma*, which means the same, suggesting that the force – or forces, for there are several in Spain – wasn't, or weren't, held in especially high regard in Hugo's entourage. I wasn't born yesterday, as you know, so I replied that although I was as clean as a whistle I felt no great respect for *los maderos* (the filth), despite the fact that my friend Harry had been one. I don't know why on earth I said that last bit – just to round off the sentence, I suppose – but when a jet of G&T emerged from Claudia's mouth I suspected that I might have put my foot in in.

"What? Does Laura know this?" she said when her mouth was empty.

"Of course."

"Are you sure?"

"Positive."

"Hmm, well, she knows what she's doing, I suppose."

I have a sixth sense for detecting anomalies and I reasoned that if Laura was merely a friend of her compatriot, Claudia oughtn't to be concerned by Harry having plodded the beat. Had I been a lesser man I might have chosen to ignore the new, shady light being cast upon Harry's chubby lover, but I'm a faithful friend and I decided to clear the matter up right away, even if it might jeopardise my chances within Hugo's outfit. Besides, if I concealed anything really shocking about Laura I knew that Harry would tear me limb from limb, as I doubted that even my blue belt in karate would be of much use were he to visit the full weight of his wrath upon me.

I sipped my drink and chuckled, my face having remained impassive while these weighty thoughts passed through my mind.

"Do you know Laura well?" I asked with insouciance.

"Not well, no."

"Her experience in the diplomatic service must be very useful to Hugo."

"Her what? Oh, no, I doubt it. I've only met her twice. She seems very nice and, as I say, she's just a friend of Hugo's, but he's a man who doesn't like to leave any loose ends." She sipped her drink and kept it down. "Come to think of it, when she did come here he didn't take her into his study or to the garage, so I expect she really is just a friend. Damn it, the drink is making me talk too much."

Feeling that I'd made all pertinent enquiries I set my mind at rest about Laura, as few people get a lie past Geoff Corless and certainly not a tipsy and not overeducated young beauty.

"Will *I* get to see inside the garage, sweetie?"

"I don't... look, forget the garage for now. Forget most of what I've said, in fact, or you'll get me into trouble with Hugo. He's warned me about prattling before."

"Very well, let's talk about us. Another drink?"

"No, you must go soon." She looked up at the darkening sky. "Very soon, in fact. Now, what else was I to ask you? Oh, yes, you said that camper van thing over there was for a friend; a French lady, I think you said."

"Er, that was the idea. Why do you ask?"

"Well, I described it to Hugo in great detail and he thinks it might be a useful vehicle for you to have."

I stroked my chin and pursed my lips. "Hmm, well, the van is mine. I'm sure my friend will be able to find another one."

"I doubt it. I've never seen anything like it before."

"Ha, yes, there are very few in Spain, if any, apart from Bambi, of course."

"Is that its name?"

"Her name, yes. If Hugo wishes I'll hang on to her for now. You can tell him that."

"I'm not to call him again before he returns."

"Where is he? What's he doing? Is he in trouble?" I asked quickly, determined to get the truth out of her.

"I cannot say. You aren't yet a trusted person."

"You won't find a more honest person than me on this side of the Pyrenees, or on the other for that matter. Another drink?" I said, deftly flicking the top off the last bottle of tonic with my lighter, a trick I'd learnt back in my Jaén days.

"Just pour that in, please. There is something that Hugo wishes you to do for him before he returns."

I nodded calmly and poured with a rock-steady hand. "Just say the word, Claudia."

"It's a very simple task. You are to drive to a little place on the coast called Valdevaqueros to pick up some goods, which you will take to Seville, a two hour drive, or maybe three in that."

"Where is Valdevaqueros? Its exact location eludes me just now."

"Near Gibraltar."

"Oh, I've just come from there," I said.

Detecting a hint of disappointment in my voice, for nobody likes to drive the same route too often, she became stern, which I found quite arousing, but by recrossing my legs I was able to stem the flow of blood.

"Listen, Geoff. This trip is no big deal. It's just a little test to make sure you're trustworthy and capable of following instructions to the letter."

"What will I be–"

She raised her dainty hand to silence me. "No questions. The less you know the better. You are an English tourist taking a holiday in your little van. From the moment you arrive in Valdevaqueros you no longer speak Spanish. I will give you your instructions and you will see no-one else from our organisation. In Seville you will receive two envelopes. One will be for you and the other for Hugo. You are to return to Torre del Mar and go to the Almanat campsite, where you will await further instructions."

"Maybe you could come and see me there, Claudia."

"It may be me who contacts you there, or someone else."

"I hope it's you. Bambi can be very cosy," I said, partly to make it clear that she was the chosen one and partly to show her I wasn't fazed by the humdrum little task that Hugo had given me.

Pretending to ignore this sexy suggestion, she pushed herself to her feet. "Come, I have to take a look inside the van before you go."

"I'll just finish my drink," I said, refreshing it.

"Take the bottle, but no drinking when you're working. Come on, it's going dark."

I followed her bouncing buttocks over to Bambi, opened the rear door, and ushered her inside.

"God, it stinks in here."

"I'll open the windows," I whispered in her ear, making her jump and then stiffen.

"Geoff, please wait outside," she said in a tremulous voice, fighting back her carnal instinct in the name of duty, so I obediently shuffled back and stepped onto the gravel.

She then examined the van closely, opening the cupboards and examining the space under the beds.

"You do have food."

"Ah, yes, I'd forgotten about Harry's emergency rations."

"Good, but when you drive to the meeting point the day after tomorrow these spaces must be empty." She straightened up. "There isn't much room in here. How on earth did three of you sleep in this thing?"

"Oh, we usually stayed in hotels, cabins and suchlike," I said, not wishing her to believe that I *enjoyed* being in such close proximity to two other men.

"I see. Look, on the trip you're going to have to put your things up front, as all the space back here will be required."

"I could put my stuff in that handy little space above the cab," I said, pointing at it.

"No, I like that space and we'll be using it, so you'll have to get rid of those camp chairs." She looked out of the side windows, then slammed the back door in my face and looked out of that window. I waved but she ignored me, so immersed was she in her task.

She opened the door and stepped out, gulping in the warm evening air.

"The back window is dark enough, but we'll have to draw the curtains on the others. Now, drive the van out and wait for me outside the gates," she said, before jogging back to the house. It was while manoeuvring Bambi out of the compound that I first gave some thought to the goods I would be transporting.

Valdevaqueros, like Gibraltar, must be close to the African coast and it occurred to me that whatever I was to transport might well come from the Dark Continent. When Claudia returned with an envelope I greeted her with a very stern expression indeed.

"Er, I won't be transporting drugs, will I?"

"No."

"Are you sure?"

"Positive. Hugo's principles don't allow him to deal in such things, so rest assured that you will never be expected to do anything like that."

"That's all right then."

The vision of Harry which had been hovering over me evaporated in an instant, to be replaced by one of a luxury sports car in which Claudia and I sat side by side, her head resting on my shoulder and her lovely hair blowing in the wind.

"Hugo led me to believe that my main job would be to drive cars from Belgium."

"Hmm, he may still require you to do that, but you'll find it far less lucrative."

"How much will I get for this first job?"

"You'll see in Seville. Here's a little money for expenses," she said, handing me an envelope which I was too polite to open. I slipped it casually into my pocket and prepared to take my leave.

"I'll be off now then," I said, moving in to plant the first of two kisses on her flawless cheeks, having decided to keep her waiting for a Geoff Corless tongue-twister.

She stepped back and raised her manicured eyebrows. "I haven't given you your instructions yet."

"Ah... I assumed they'd be in the envelope."

"Don't be stupid. We never write anything down and rarely use phones. Keep yours switched off once you begin the job. Now listen carefully."

"I'm all ears."

"You are to arrive in Valdevaqueros at exactly 1400 hours on Friday, the day after tomorrow."

"Roger."

"What?"

"Nothing. Do go on."

"You are to make your way towards a bar called Tangana, down a little lane to the sea. You are to leave the van in a public carpark just before the bar and some bungalows. You are to leave the key under the driver's mat and spend about one hour in the bar, after which you will return to the van, retrieve the key from under the mat, and drive away in the direction of Cádiz. Is that clear so far?"

"As crystal."

"The contents of the van are of no concern of yours and you must pay no attention to them whatsoever. Is *that* clear?"

"As a bell."

"What?"

"Extremely clear."

"Make sure you have enough petrol, and water to drink, because you mustn't stop before reaching Seville, where you will go to Los Arcos shopping centre. This is very easy to find as you will see signs for it before entering the city."

"I'll look it up on my phone."

"You will *not* look it up on your phone, silly, or anything else concerning the trip. Remember, you're a foreign tourist, so you can ask directions in Valdevaqueros, in English, and only an idiot could miss the signs to the shopping centre in Seville. There you park in a quiet spot on the large carpark and leave the key under the mat again. That's the beauty of your van, you see, that our contacts cannot miss it. Once again you will go away for one hour, before returning to the van, where you will find two envelopes under the cushions of the left-hand bed, one for you and one for Hugo. Then you are free to make your way back to Torre del Mar, but please check into the Almanat campsite by Sunday evening. On Monday morning you must stay near the van, as I or somebody else will come to collect Hugo's money, which you must guard with your life until then. Is that clear, Geoff?"

"Perfectly."

"Repeat it to me then."

I repeated it, more or less word-for-word, apart from having forgotten the name of the place in Valdevaqueros and the shopping centre, so she repeated the whole spiel, before making me repeat it repeatedly, by which time it was pitch dark and I was dying for a wee.

"Go now, and keep repeating the names of the places you must go to. Good luck," she said, extending her hand, which I shook quickly before saluting, hopping into the van, and driving as far as some trees, where I leapt out and syphoned the python in the nick of time.

It being ten o'clock by then I decided it was too late to look for a campsite, so I simply pulled over in a handy layby on the narrow lane and climbed into my living quarters. After mixing a can of chilli con carne with another of spaghetti hoops, for I was famished by then, I heated it up and scoffed it out of the pan, before mixing a malt whisky and water and lying down on the bed under which my first pay packet was to be deposited. That reminded me of my expenses money and I was pleased to find that Claudia had given me €400, no less than I deserved, for I had an inkling that my mission wasn't an altogether legal one, but as I'd been assured that no heinous substances were involved I didn't intend to lose much sleep over it.

3

I slept like a log until about 6.00am, when a blaring horn awoke me. On peering through the curtain I spied a huge tractor waiting to enter the gate which I was blocking, so I jumped out, hotfooted it round to the driver's door and sped away. While breakfasting in a bar on the outskirts of Torre del Mar I decided I might as well cover some of the ground to Valdevaqueros that day, so by noon I had checked into a campsite near the beach beyond Estepona, where I had a much needed shower and washed some clothes, but not my suit, of course, which would be dry-cleaned or simply replaced by a couple of lighter ones, depending on how much I earned from my driving job.

The campsite was busy and as I relaxed in my remaining chair, having dumped the other two near the toilets, I received the glad eye from several tasty young chicks, but though I returned their amorous glances I told myself that the last thing I needed was a night of unbridled passion before the big day. After a swim in the sea and another in the pool I enjoyed a restorative siesta before cooking up a dinner of tinned macaroni cheese and meatballs, before electing to jettison most of the remaining tins, as although I'm a naturally thrifty person there was no need to deny myself wholesome restaurant meals. After a small malt whisky I opened all the windows and retired early, having concluded that I liked my new lifestyle very much indeed.

The following morning I left the site at ten and drove to the end of the motorway at Algeciras, after which I dawdled along the picturesque main road, stopping here and there to kill some time. It was only when driving into Valdevaqueros that I began to feel a tad nervous, but I parked the van in the agreed spot and sauntered towards the bar, before rushing back with the ignition key and shoving it under the mat. The Tangana proved to be a *chiringuito*, or mostly open-air bar, and a spacious one at that, so it wasn't difficult to maintain a measure of anonymity while I ate a sandwich and completely blanked out the scantily clad girls who just *happened* to pass my table, sometimes more than once. After taking coffee I ordered a large bottle of water and paid the bill, before visiting the bathroom and making ready to return to Bambi. Despite drying my hands thoroughly they soon became damp again, and though the day was hot and humid I couldn't deny the fact that my impending haulage mission was giving me a touch of the jitters. I mean, though drugs had been ruled out, for all I knew I was about to transport a consignment of diamonds, or a case of uranium en route to North Korea, so it was only natural that I should be a little anxious, I told myself when Bambi came into view, looking slightly lower on her axles than when I had left her.

As she had been parked at a slightly different angle I concluded that my associates had driven her away to load her up, and when I hopped into the cab I couldn't resist glancing through the thin curtain to see what was on board. I saw only plain brown boxes piled about four feet high and felt within my rights to peek into the nearest box. A wave of relief washed over me when I found cartons of cigarettes inside. Ha, I should have guessed, as tobacco smuggling is a widespread, harmless pastime in the environs of Gibraltar, so when I started her up and eased out of the carpark I felt that Claudia's pedantic briefing had been a little excessive and Machiavellian, as this was child's play to a man like me.

When I joined the flow of traffic towards Cádiz I was surprised how sluggishly Bambi accelerated, but I reasoned that if you pack enough light boxes into a vehicle they add up to a considerable load. Luckily the road was busy and we seldom exceeded sixty k.p.h. so I switched on the radio and settled down to enjoy the trip. It was while singing along to *Hotel California* that I first heard a strange noise. I know the song well and couldn't recall any throat clearing, so I assumed it must be a live version and thought no more of it. After an endless series of adverts they played *A Whiter Shade of Pale* and when I heard a soft but sonorous farting sound I reached the immediate and inevitable conclusion that something besides cigarettes was in the back of Bambi.

Despite the heat I immediately broke out in a cold sweat and began to conjecture about what or who was buried back there under the boxes. I recalled Claudia's words about paying no attention to my cargo, so I turned up the radio and pressed on past the white hilltop village of Vejer de la Frontera, whose beauty I completely failed to appreciate, before joining a motorway and becoming rather paranoid about the stares and occasional pips I received from passing motorists, nothing new when driving Bambi, but especially annoying when pouring with sweat, despite the open windows. When a *Guardia Civil* car began to pass slowly by I dried my left temple with my t-shirt sleeve and stared intently ahead, and I think it was then that it dawned on me that earning money in this way was fraught with peril. The police car forged ahead, but left me with a tremendous urge to pee, so at the next exit I left the motorway, pulled over, and relieved myself behind a tree.

This was near a place called Patria and I decided to stay off the motorway and follow the parallel main road until I had calmed down. After trundling along behind a lorry for a while my pulse rate finally dropped into double figures and I told myself that in two hours I would be leaving Bambi in the shopping centre carpark, before returning to find her empty, apart from two envelopes under the bed, both of which I hoped would be pretty damn thick after what I was going through. As my live cargo made no further noises I soon began to forget about him/her/it/them and when I rejoined the motorway after a few miles my agile mind was able to view the situation in a whole new light. When I thought about the tales I'd have to tell – in the distant future, of course – all trace of my fleeting feeling of unease evaporated and was replaced by one verging on euphoria.

Who would have thought that only three months earlier I had been forced to humour drunken businessmen at the bar of the mediocre hotel where I had worked four or five nights a week, and now here I was, blazing a trail across Andalucía in Bambi with who knows who or what on board? Might there be a couple of rare African mammals back there? Or, more likely, a brave political exile or two? I turned the radio off to listen for clues and began to think it a pity that Claudia had given me strict instructions to pay no attention to my cargo, words whose true significance I now understood.

On passing Chiclana de la Frontera my feeling of pride and elation slowly turned into one of indignation. Who did this Hugo fellow take me for? A mere flunky who would blindly do his boss's bidding at great peril to himself without having the slightest clue as to what he was transporting along a busy motorway in broad daylight? Had my forbears built the greatest empire in the world, including Gibraltar, for me to be reduced to the role of a blinkered courier for a *Belgian*? Besides, how could I tell my tales of derring-do if I didn't know what the hell I was carrying? What would I tell Harry, for example, when my days of toiling for Hugo were but a distant memory.

'One time I carried a live cargo to Seville at great risk to myself,' I might say to him.

'Oh, what? Who? Do tell,' he would reply, all ears.

'I don't know, I never found out, but I heard a fart.'

(Cackles of condescending laughter followed by sundry scathing comments.)

No, no, no, I concluded that this simply wouldn't do, so when a service station sign appeared I left the slipstream of an olive oil tanker and headed off the motorway. The service station turned out to be just a petrol station, so I parked behind a lorry and trotted round to the back door. It was with some trepidation that I turned the handle, only to find it locked, but on retrieving the key I opened up and scoured the sea of boxes that filled Bambi to about 85% of her capacity. On tiptoe I gingerly lifted a couple of them, but saw only more boxes, and not wishing to unload the entire consignment I resorted to clearing my throat, hoping, I suppose, that the occupant(s) would reciprocate in some way and give me an indication as to their species and whereabouts. On hearing no response I then tried saying hello in four or five languages, but my polyglottic greeting likewise failed to elicit a response, and it was only on beginning to close the door, fearing that I may have been deluding myself all along, that I saw a face staring down at me from the space over the cab.

It was a bearded black face, peering at me from under a dark sheet, with large staring eyes and a lot of white teeth, bared not in a smile of welcome but an angry grimace.

"Hello," I said.

"Drive, man, drive!" the man replied in a hoarse whisper, before pulling the sheet over his head and groaning.

"Are you comfortable?" I asked, because if the size of his body corresponded to that of his face it must have been a tight squeeze for him up there, though Harry had managed it during one childish episode on the trip that now seemed like a lifetime ago.

"Drive, man, drive!" he repeated in an exasperated tone, so I closed the door, hopped back into the cab, and got back on the road.

Ha, so that was why Bambi felt a tad top-heavy, I mused as I slotted myself into the slow lane, before the realisation of what I had just witnessed hit me like a ton of bricks. The man was almost certainly an African and if he wasn't riding up front with me it could only mean one thing; that he oughtn't to be travelling along a Spanish road, therefore he was an illegal immigrant. The old cold sweat broke out once again on realising what a pickle I might be getting myself into as, unlike cigarette smugglers, people traffickers are viewed in a rather dim light nowadays. This second minor panic attack, however, proved to be more short-lived than the first as it dawned on me that only an hour separated me from the Seville shopping centre where I would walk away from Bambi and her mixed cargo, drink a beer or two, and return to find the reward for my audacious assignment under the left-hand bed. Besides, as the big black man was presumably happy to be in Europe, despite his unfriendly greeting, it was a 'win win' situation for both of us, as I firmly believe that everybody has the right to better themselves, just as I was doing, assuming I didn't get stopped by the police and thrown into prison.

I kept my cool pretty well on that final leg, partly thanks to a spell of hypothesising on the past and future of my precious load. In all likelihood my travelling companion would soon make it to an accommodating country, such as Britain, where he would work and send money to his impoverished relatives back home or, better still, have them come over to join him, something that wouldn't please Harry, a latent racist, but which I considered a well-deserved end to a journey which was probably, all things considered, even more harrowing than my own. As I drove along with the big fellow directly above my head I restrained an impulse to shout up words of encouragement and when we finally arrived at the shopping centre – which, like Claudia had said, was easy to find – I would have dearly loved to help him down from his cubbyhole and maybe hand him a few notes from my envelope, but as that couldn't be I left the key under the mat and walked away from one of the most exciting events of my life, barring certain sexual encounters, resigned to not seeing that brave man emerge from Bambi on his way to a better life.

On leaving the carpark, however, I spotted a few handy trees and decided to conceal myself behind one of them to observe the denouement of my daring deed. I chose this impulsive course of action with future storytelling once more in mind, as when I eventually told Harry, Jeremy or whoever about my exploit it would be nice to put a body to a face, so to speak, lest it appear that I was merely a clueless driver rather than an emancipator of those less fortunate than ourselves. After a few minutes spent nonchalantly reading number plates I looked up to see a large blue van reverse into the space directly behind Bambi and two hefty young fellows wearing casual clothes and baseball caps hop out of the passenger door. They then opened both rear doors and stood between them, upon which the driver reversed a tad more, effectively obscuring the view from either side; a shrewd move which I added to my mental box of tricks, though the fact that Bambi had just one rear door meant that I wouldn't be able to emulate them in my trusty little camper.

My admiration immediately gave way to annoyance, however, as all I could see from my vantage point were the calves and feet of the men who appeared to be transferring the boxes to their van. I soon found myself leaving the sanctuary of the tree and creeping towards the scene, part of my brain egging me on while another part urged me to get the hell out of there until they had finished. I guess courage is a subconscious sort of thing and my desire to catch a glimpse of the human portion of my load drove my feet ever closer, until I found myself about a yard away, peering through the narrow gap between blue door and whitish bodywork. I was rewarded by a glimpse of a stocky young black man dressed in shorts and a t-shirt being helped up into the van, and I was about to withdraw when to my immense surprise a slim black *lady* followed him, carrying a *baby*, which she then passed to her presumed partner, before being hoisted aboard.

Feeling that I would dine out on this astounding story for quite a while, I began to back away from the vans, but my retreat was arrested by the firm clasp of a burly forearm around my neck. I know several karate moves which would have enabled me to reduce my assailant to a quivering wretch, but none of them sprang to mind at the time, and besides, this was one of my associates I was dealing with and Hugo wouldn't appreciate me rendering him unfit for duty for many weeks. So, having decided to remain calm and concentrate on breathing through the sliver of windpipe which was still open, I allowed him to guide me past the van door and escort me into the back of Bambi, where he pulled me down beside him on the right-hand bench and left his arm draped affectionately over my shoulder. In the meantime the other two chaps had finished loading the van, so they closed the doors, before joining us and occupying the opposite bench, which reminded me of certain rainy episodes during my trip with Harry and Jeremy, except in this case there were three of them and none of them looked especially chummy.

"What you see?" the driver said in heavily accented and ungrammatical Spanish.

"Me? Nothing," I replied with an endearing chuckle.

"What you do?" said one of the other chaps.

"Shopping," I said, pointing towards the commercial centre.

The driver then gave me a playful shove which caused me to bump my head on the wall, before conferring with his compadres in a language which I couldn't quite place. I was torn between Belarusian and Ukrainian, though it could just as easily have been Latvian or Estonian, but before I could hazard a guess they had finished their chinwag and were all looking at me, one glowering, one scowling, and the third just gazing gloomily.

"You come with us," this last chap said.

"I have my own van," I said.

"You come with us," he repeated.

"What will happen to me?" I asked out of idle curiosity.

"I don't know. Our boss decide. Maybe he feed you to pigs," he said, cackling insanely and baring a couple of gold teeth rather like Freya's.

"Maybe you go *long* swim," said the fellow opposite me, nudging his bench companion.

"Or maybe we just shoot you," said the more sullen of the three, which made us all laugh until he pulled his jacket aside to reveal a small gun in a leather holster, after which my mirth deserted me, though they carried on sniggering for a while.

Suspecting that they might be at least half-serious about my impending demise, I decided to try to keep the conversation flowing in the hope of eventually cajoling them into letting me go.

"That's a nice van you have there. Is it a Volkswagen?"

"Hmm, turbo-diesel," said the driver.

"Hire van," said the advocate of drowning at sea.

"Shut up," said the sullen one. "Now you go quietly into van."

"But I prefer mine," I said, patting the cushion.

That innocent pat certainly grabbed their attention, so when I saw six eyes focussed on the back of my hand I decided to pat some more for good measure.

"This *your* van?" asked the gunslinger, his shallow brow furrowing like a recently ploughed field.

"Of course. She's called Bambi."

"You lie," said the driver, that beefy forearm of his looming ever closer.

"It is, really."

They exchanged perplexed glances, before looking at me and seeing a face of such fearless innocence that they all began to shake their heads, though the sullen one wasn't quite convinced.

"You prove it," he said in a challenging sort of way.

"Er, there's a camp chair up front, and two travel bags with clothes, and a pillow and sheets."

"And? What else?" he said, his narrow eyes becoming more slit-like than ever.

"And... and... a guitar. Yes, under that bench. I know Claudia told me to leave them empty but that guitar's really dear to me and I simply couldn't throw it away. I don't have a television, you see, so it helps me to while away the evenings. Sorry about that. I hope it didn't take up too much space for cigarettes or... er, babies."

Another conflab ensued, during which I heard the name Claudia at least twice, so I felt pretty sure I was out of the woods.

"I've been to Hugo's house near Torre del Mar," I added for good measure, which rather than producing the laughter and backslapping that I'd anticipating, made them all shake their heads and utter various groaning, sighing and tutting sounds.

"I'm Geoff," I said, offering my hand to the driver.

"Tú eres un gran hijo de la gran puta," he replied, and I reproduce this in Spanish for the simple reason that it was the first wholly correct sentence that any of them had uttered. It means, 'You are a great son of the great whore,' by the way, but he shook my hand all the same, and I must say he had a heck of a grip.

The gunman then opened the back door and they began to squeeze out, so I decided to stay there chilling out for a while after they'd gone, because all in all it had been a trying time. The driver was the last to leave and on stepping down he turned round, put his hand inside his jacket, and extracted two envelopes, which he dropped unceremoniously on the floor.

"Oh, thanks."

He grunted and gripped the door handle.

"Oh, I say, there's really no need to mention this misunderstanding to Claudia or Hugo, is there?" I said, but he merely rolled his eyes and slammed the door.

When the turbo-diesel van had roared away I sat quietly for a while taking stock of the situation. As far as I could see I had made only one minor error, that of approaching the vans, and I concluded that as curiosity had come disturbingly close to killing the cat I ought to refrain from such nosiness on future missions. This then raised the question in my mind of if I might have jeopardised said future missions by not obeying my instructions to the letter. Would my (probably) Slavic co-workers feel the need to inform Hugo, Claudia or whoever their contact was of my minor transgression, or would the three of them just put it down to inexperience and keep shtum on my behalf?

That remained to be seen, as did the contents of my envelope, as if I felt my remuneration insufficient it might be me kicking Hugo's organisation into touch rather than the other way round. The larger, fatter envelope had nothing at all written on it – a canny precaution – and on the other a capital letter G had been inscribed in pencil. I thought G as good a codename as any, though I'd have preferred one composed of numbers, like 008 or something, and as I slowly broke the seal I speculated as to the likely amount of money concealed therein. I hoped to find at least a grand, as not just anyone has the nerve required for that risky cross-country dash, but as I'd already received four hundred up front I had an inkling that another six hundred might await me. On finally counting the numerous used fifty euro notes I was pleasantly surprised to find a total of three thousand euros (€3000) within that nondescript envelope, upon which I gave a whoop of joy, before clamping a hand over my mouth, as I was still at the scene of the handover.

This was good news indeed and I surmised that it surely meant that the three blokes believed I had carried out my mission almost flawlessly and that they would overlook my slight security lapse when reporting back to base. This minor matter bugged me, you see, as although I'd only met Hugo once, when he'd been bonhomie incarnate, I couldn't help recalling a certain icy glint in his blue Belgian eyes which suggested that were one to let him down he might turn a touch nasty. That day at his house, of course, I hadn't known that he had at least one posse of East-Europeans under his command, so the perceptive reader will no doubt comprehend the feeling of disquiet which took the edge off my delight at receiving such a handsome sum.

But not for long, as on inserting the wad of notes into my wallet I reflected that I would have had to graft at that crummy Kendal hotel for about ten weeks to earn an amount which I had made in a few hours, so on the whole I was pretty pleased with myself and felt that I deserved some sort of treat. Thus it was that after transferring my belonging to the back of Bambi I crammed my sweaty wool suit into a plastic bag and tossed it into a waste bin, before trotting over to the shopping centre to buy myself a new one. In a modern gent's outfitters on the second floor I summoned over a dishy little assistant and told her that although I normally purchased made-to-measure suits, I hoped to find a quality lightweight number among her large and varied collection.

"They're not mine," she said, a little snottily, before prancing over to a nearby rack. "These are linen. Take your pick."

The uppity wench wasn't to know that I had the wherewithal to whisk her away for a luxuriously passionate weekend, as I didn't look especially affluent in my crumpled casual clothes, so I decided to give her one last chance.

"I don't *need* to purchase made-to-measure suits of course, as my bodily proportions are considered ideal, so off-the-rack stuff is practically made for me," I said with a crafty smile and a cheeky wink.

She turned away and rustled in the rack. "This one is size forty-six, thirty-six in English," she said, proffering a lightweight light-blue suit.

"Ha, what makes you think I want to know the English size, dear?"

"Because from your accent I presume you to be a foreigner."

"A foreigner?"

"Yes."

"But not necessarily English?"

She looked at me rather like my colleague had done on closing Bambi's door and said that she didn't know and was I going to buy a suit or what?

"Not until you guess where I'm from," I said in my best Andaluz accent.

She puffed out her cheeks and looked at her feet, or my feet, before raising her eyes to meet mine and venturing a smile for the first time.

"I think you are from Malaga. You are either a flamenco guitarist or a bullfighter, I'm not sure which."

"Ha, not a bad guess! I'm from Jaén, more or less, and I'm a guitarist, but more contemporary than flamenco, though I do dabble in that too," I said, striking a pose and finger-picking the air.

"How about this beige suit?" she said, whipping one out with a flamencoesque flourish.

"Size thirty-six... er forty-six, you say? I think my shoulders are too wide for that."

"Try it on over there."

I did her bidding and found it to be a perfect fit, so I imagine that Spanish sizes are bigger than ours, as I normally wear a forty (English), though I once filled out to a forty-four after a winter of weight training and a course of vitamin pills supplied to me by my colossal coach.

"It looks good," she said after I'd catwalked back from the cubicle.

"How about dinner tonight?" I span around on the heels of my sandals and faced her again. "At the best place in town," I added.

"How about a couple of shirts to go with the suit?" she asked, clearly mulling over my offer.

Half an hour later I walked out of there with the beige suit, three shirts, two ties, two vests, six pairs of boxer shorts, four of socks, a belt, a box of silk handkerchiefs, an expensive pair of sunglasses, a panama hat and a promise that she'd call me when she finished work at nine. On returning to Bambi, however, I felt the irresistible pull of the open road and as I wasn't 100% sure that she hadn't been stringing me along I decided to forsake her and head back towards the coast. After a momentary panic on failing to locate Hugo's envelope – it was under the sink – I lobbed it into the space over the cab and made ready to leave.

It's curious how one's reaction to events are often delayed, as it wasn't until I had travelled several miles down the road to Malaga that upon reviewing my misunderstanding with the three hoodlums I broke out into one of my annoyingly habitual cold sweats. When I had calmed down and dried up I reflected that although my life had so far been a varied and in some ways exciting one, I had never crossed over the line into lawlessness, not for want of nerve, but due to the fact that no illicit but lucrative business schemes had been proposed to me before. It wasn't, however, too late to chuck this whole Hugo thing and steer myself and Bambi out of harm's way. I glanced up at the roof, above which lay an envelope whose girth suggested that many thousands of euros lay within, so what was to stop me from heading north, ditching Bambi – a sad thought – and making a new life for myself elsewhere?

After at least an hour of internal debate, during which time I thrashed out the matter in the dialectic style of Plato, I reached the conclusion that there was one major stumbling block preventing me from taking all the cash – which I'd earned, in a way – and scarpering; namely Harry. Over the years Harry has often poured scorn on my schemes to better myself, such as the time I looked into breeding Savannah Monitor lizards in my flat, or my proposal that the three of us should invest in a massage parlour which I would manage, though in each case it was Jeremy's judicious advice that made me desist. Now, though unwittingly, Harry was throwing a spanner into my works once more. If I pocketed Hugo's ill-earned spoils the Belgian would immediately ask his friend Laura to find out where the hell I'd got to, upon which she would inform Harry of my disappearance with the loot.

Being an ex-copper and wannabe detective – though he had never made the grade – instead of turning a blind eye he would probably set out to track me down, as Laura – the nature of whose association with Hugo was yet to be determined, though I'd begun to doubt her squeaky-clean diplomatic background – would be liable to omit the fact that Hugo had tricked me into people smuggling, either because she was in cahoots with him or simply didn't have a clue about the illicit nature of his enterprise. By the time I reached Antequera these and many other thoughts had been processed by my analytical brain and I decided that, all things considered, I'd better stick to Plan H for the time being – Plan Hugo – rather than triggering Plan B – Plan Bugger Off – which I might be executing shortly in any case if news of my indiscretion got back to the Belgian.

I stayed at the best hotel in Antequera that night and cut quite a dash in my new suit, as the other guests were all as sloppily attired as one has come to expect these days. Rocío, the silly shopgirl in Seville, failed to call me, probably preferring to eat a takeaway pizza with a pimply boyfriend than share my platter of roast suckling pig, washed down with a fine bottle of *Ribera del Duero* red, but our lives are full of missed opportunities, even mine, as on handling Hugo's envelope, now in my room for safekeeping, I could only sigh wistfully on reflecting that my innate honesty prevented me from fleecing the shadowy Belgian.

4

The following morning, after a leisurely breakfast and a stroll around the not unattractive town, I decided to stay for another night, so it was on Sunday morning when I headed down towards the coast, taking a picturesque cross-country route and stopping off for lunch in the village of Riogordo. As I piloted Bambi past a large reservoir and down the well-surfaced road to the coast I looked forward to reaching the campsite and plunging into the sea, before stretching out on my towel and topping up my already impressive tan. I had the rest of the day to relax and resolved to put the following day's meeting with Claudia, or whoever, out of my mind, as when it did occasionally enter it my skin became absurdly goosepimpled and I found myself humming tunelessly, rather like Harry did when it was his turn to pay for a round of drinks.

On entering the Almanat campsite to the west of Torre del Mar I was surprised to see a couple of kids, a boy and a girl, wandering along in the altogether, and I thought it remarkably progressive of their parents to allow them to enjoy their natural nakedness for a few years longer than usual, until one of the parents, a paunchy fellow of forty, fell in with them, he too wearing nothing more than a pair of flip-flops. For a moment I became mesmerised by the curiously rhythmical side-to-side motion of his pendulous member, until a huge pair of breasts emerged from behind a cabin, closely followed by the rest of an amply proportioned matron, similarly unattired.

This place, I concluded, was a nudist, or naturist, campsite and my initial inclination was to turn tail – no pun intended, as I was still fully clothed – and head elsewhere, not because I'm ashamed of my body, far from it, but because, well, I just wasn't used to seeing all that uncovered flesh loping around. If all the women there were like that hefty matriarch I foresaw no danger of my blood flowing where it oughtn't, but the first tidy piece I saw without a stitch on would almost certainly send my unfailing but unruly John Thomas skywards, causing consternation and, I feared, instant expulsion, thus incurring the wrath of Claudia, or whoever, if she/he found me waiting conspicuously outside the gates of that Garden of Eden the following morning. So, I parked Bambi, hurried into reception and told the mercifully partly-clad young lady what I required.

"I'm sorry, at this time of year you must stay for at least four nights," said the slim, good-natured girl whose flimsy long white t-shirt was already causing a vague stirring down there, the effect being even more arousing than if she'd been starkers, I suspect.

"But… well, I'm not sure if I'll like it yet."

She smiled placidly. "Have you never been to a naturist campsite before?"

"No, and, well, to be frank, I'm a bit worried about how my… er, libido will react to the unaccustomed… er, stimuli," I said, just like that, as I'm not ashamed to admit that my nerves were getting the better of me, even more, believe it or not, than when I was being threatened with execution in the back of Bambi.

"Don't worry, just wear your swim shorts until you feel comfortable. Men often have that fear, but it never happens." Her pretty face clouded. "Except once, last year, but he did it on purpose." The cloud cleared. "So, shall I book you in for four nights?"

"I don't know. I was once diagnosed with an excess of testosterone, you see," I said, which though not strictly true was, I felt, as good an alibi as any and ought to prevent me from being arrested if she were wrong, as though my member is a modest piece when flaccid, it swells to alarming proportions when aroused, so even in swim shorts I'd be liable to stand out from the crowd, so to speak, if seen in profile, but I don't suppose you really need to know this.

She gazed at me pensively for a while, before clicking her fingers and smiling again. "Look, go and park up on one of the empty pitches and see how you feel about it. Have a wander round and if you still feel uncomfortable just pop in to tell me on your way out."

"OK, I'll give it a try," I said, resisting an absurd urge to pat my packet.

In the event, once I'd parked up and had a mosey round I realised that all that naked flesh, a small proportion of it delectable, wasn't producing the effect I'd feared, so, clad only in my skimpy swim shorts and sandals I returned to reception with my wallet.

"How's it going?" said the charming, sympathetic girl.

"Great, no problem so far. I'll stay for four nights."

"Lovely. That'll be €96."

"Fine. Ha, the only thing around here that's bulging is my wallet," I said as I slapped it (the wallet) on the counter.

Her brow creased on hearing this witticism and after receiving the notes in silence she pushed four coins towards me.

"Oh, do keep that," I said, and something about the way she regarded me, with a faint frown and narrowed eyes, made me desist from inviting her out for the evening, as I didn't wish my advances to be spurned twice in two days, something that had rarely happened before.

"Thanks. Enjoy your stay," she said rather mechanically, so I wiggled my bottom on the way out to cheer her up.

I then made a beeline for the beach, dumped my towel and sun cream, and ran into the sea, from where I observed that on the entire section of sand not a single person was wearing anything more substantial than a baseball cap. Plucking up my courage I slipped off my shorts and splashed around for a while, subtly nearing a young couple who were playing catch, just to make sure that my tackle would behave itself. I obliquely watched the young lady jump into the air to catch the ball, her firm breasts bouncing in an appealing way, and on slipping my hand under the water I was relieved to note no telltale swelling. I stuck around to watch her receive a few more passes, just to be on the safe side, but when the muscular chap glared at me and tensed his muscles I swam away employing a brisk crawl, before leaving the water some way away, spinning my shorts nonchalantly as I wandered back to my towel.

I then set about catching a few rays, but when it came to applying sun cream I was reluctant to rub it on my shrivelled schlong, for obvious reasons, so I spent most of the time on my belly. Besides, when I did lie on my back I found myself constantly peering down to check on my faithful friend, so after a while I got so fed up of the whole thing that I slipped on my shorts, had a dip in the pool, returned to Bambi, donned my new suit and walked into town. By then it was the hour of the *paseo*, or evening stroll, so I joined the mainly Spanish strollers on the promenade, tipping my hat to any young chicks who looked my way. Most of them appeared to have eyes for me, so when I tired of hat tipping I wiggled my sunglasses instead, and I was delighted that my new look was having such an effect on the ladies, though it has to be said that few people passed by without ogling me, including old men, young children and three nuns, so after a while I began to feel as conspicuous as I had on the beach. Clothing-wise it's so hard to get the balance right these days, I reflected as I sipped beer and munched a few tapas, so concerned about staining my suit that I swore not to wear it again until I went out on my next date with a pretty young thing, something I felt was long overdue, as what with one thing and another it had been a while since I'd wined and dined a dame, not to mention putting Percy through his paces, though I might well be seeing Claudia the next day, so when I handed over Hugo's dosh I'd carry on where I'd left off after our intimate soiree at our boss's house.

***

"Buenos días, Claudia, cariño," I said at ten the next morning as I pushed myself out of my camp chair to greet her. I was wearing shorts and a vest, as I wasn't sure if she knew about this nudism business and I didn't want to alarm her.

"Get in the van, you bloody clown," she said, or words to that effect, so I opened the back door and ushered her inside, before closing it behind me, sitting down opposite her and getting a distinctly *déjà vu* feeling, as she looked every bit as grim as those three fellows back in Seville. From the head down she looked ravishing in a loose sleeveless top, no bra, short white shorts and sandals but, as I say, from the expression on her face you'd have thought she'd just swallowed a mouthful of seawater, though her silky dark hair was as lovely as ever.

"You didn't tell me this was a nudist campsite," I said with an impish smile, hoping to lighten proceedings.

"I didn't know. Hugo told me to send you here."

"Ha, he certainly has a sense of humour, the old devil," I said with a hearty laugh.

"Not anymore, he hasn't. What you did in Seville could have put the whole operation in jeopardy, *gilipollas*," she growled, that last word meaning 'daft one' or, in northern England, 'pillock'.

"Well, I just wanted to make sure things were going all right."

"You standing there gawping could have attracted a security guard."

"I'd have distracted him. That's another reason I approached the vans," I said, thinking on my feet.

"If one had raised the alarm they would have shot him. Do you realise that, you damn numbskull? You would have had blood on your hands."

"Not if I didn't touch the corpse," I said with a chuckle, still intent on diffusing her anger, a tactic I'd employed several times in the past when one of my lovers had discovered the existence of another, but seldom, I admit, with much success.

"My God, you're more of an idiot than I thought, Geoff. Hugo was pretty pissed off when they told him and he asked me to see just how repentant you felt about your stupid blunder, as he's a reasonable man, deep down. So what do I tell him? That you merely joked about a mistake that could have cost him thousands?"

I looked suitably contrite, but couldn't resist one more joke, as Claudia's furious face was making me feel horny.

"Oh, yes, about that envelope."

"What?"

"Well, on Friday I took it to my hotel room for safekeeping, but when I returned after dinner it had gone."

Claudia blanched so much that she went from looking like a Caribbean beauty to a Lancaster chip shop employee in an instant.

"Not to worry though. He can have my money instead. It was my fault after all."

"You cannot be serious," she said hoarsely.

"Afraid so," I said with a shrug, doing my damnedest not to laugh.

"There was forty thousand in that envelope."

"What?" I cried, momentarily mortified, as when I play a role I put my whole heart and soul into it.

"You're a dead man, Geoff."

I stroked my bronzed legs, before snapping out of my histrionic trance. I looked up sheepishly. "I was… er, joking, Claudia."

She silently scanned my face and the blood slowly returned to hers. "Give me the envelope," she murmured.

"Sure," I said, standing to reach into the space above the cab. I had to paw around for quite a while before I found it, but there it was, so I hopped off the bed, sat down and handed it over. She slit it open with a lacquered fingernail and removed the yellowy €200 notes, which she counted adroitly, before slipping them back into the envelope and popping it into her leather handbag.

"All's well that ends well, eh?" I said, with a winsome smile.

By way of reply she leant forward and punched me on the nose.

"Ouch!" I said, before the appalling pain reduced me to silence. That slim right arm certainly packs a punch, I thought as I viewed her through teary eyes, her own eyes somewhat softened after her cathartic wallop. "I suppose I deserved that," I uttered in a curiously nasal voice.

"You're bleeding," she said, reaching for a tissue near my pillow.

"Not that one!"

"Why not?"

"It's… snotty. Kitchen towel under sink."

She handed me the roll and I stemmed the flow. She looked at me pityingly before kneading her noble brow and sighing. "Sorry about that. If you knew Hugo as I do you wouldn't have joked about the money. I'm going to get some air and have a think," she said, before heading for the door, returning to grab her handbag, and leaving the van.

When she returned a few minutes later she seemed much recovered and even managed a smile.

"You look like a walrus, Geoff."

"Why? Oh, I see," I said, fingering the twisted kitchen towels that I'd shoved up my nostrils, partly, I admit, to elicit her sympathy after the impulsive jab that I could see she already regretted. Had I not been such a gentleman she would have still been out cold, but her radical method of letting off steam seemed to have cleared the air, so I thought it was time to talk about my next assignment.

"When's my next job?" I asked after removing my tusks.

"Are you serious?"

"Deadly."

"What?"

"Very."

She sighed and shook her lovely head, before gazing into my now tear-free eyes. "I'm not sure there'll be another job, Geoff. All I can do is tell Hugo that you're very sorry about what you did in Seville. I'll… I'll tell him that you didn't know there was another man in the van, so you thought you ought to keep an eye on things. Being overzealous is no bad thing, so he might buy that, and he'll be so happy to receive the money that he might give you a second chance."

"When's he coming back?"

"Soon, I think, as it was this money he was waiting for," she said, patting her handbag.

"Cash flow problems, eh? I had those at the hotel too," I said, which was true, as that damned computerised bar till never seemed to tally.

"Precisely. Once I've paid that... Axel, he'll come home," she said with a shudder.

"Bad sort this Axel fellow, is he?"

"Makes Hugo look like a choirboy, but there I go again, talking too much. You have that effect on me, Geoff. Whenever I'm with you I cannot seem to take things seriously."

"Hmm, I expect we're soulmates or something," I said, stroking my tender conk.

She shuddered again, no doubt thinking about that devil Axel.

"Listen, Claudia, isn't there anything I can do to get this Axel beast off Hugo's back?"

Wide-eyed with admiration, she was momentarily speechless, so I strove to clarify my far from idle offer.

"If you tell me where he lives, I could... spook him."

"Spook him?"

"Yes, I could... er, dress up as a policeman and hang around, you know."

"He'd feed you to the pigs."

"Hmm, pigs were mentioned in Bambi back in Seville."

"Axel really has some. People have disappeared. You don't need to be a genius to put two and two together. Forget his name and *don't* mention him in Hugo's presence."

"Righty-ho. So, when do I see him?"

"I don't know yet. Stay here for a few days and I'll contact you."

"Er, do you mind awfully if I change campsite?"

"Do you not like it here?"

"No, I consider it... undignified to wander around with my... thing banging against my thighs," I said, before a cunning thought struck me. "We could just go for a quick nude swim together, then I'll check out."

She smiled and narrowed her exquisite eyes. "Hmm, that's tempting, because I did see a couple of lovely bodies just now."

I stroked my left bicep with my right hand, pushing it up in the process. I raised my eyebrows and gave her my best 'come hither' look.

"Yes," she went on. "One Scandinavian girl really took my fancy. Such long legs and slim hips."

She licked her lips, so I licked mine, until I twigged.

"What? You like women?"

"Oh, yes. Did you not guess?"

"Well, no, but I'm sure if I were a woman I'd like women too. Shall we go and find her and try to tempt her back to Bambi?"

She shook her head. "You don't understand, Geoff. I *only* like women, in that way."

"Oh, I thought you liked me," I said, remembering her smouldering glances at Hugo's house.

"I do like you, Geoff, despite being such a chump, or maybe because you're such a chump, but I'm just not sexually attracted to men."

"Not even me?"

"No, I'm afraid not. It's true that you do have a strong feminine side, much more so than most men, but even so... To be honest, at first I thought you might be gay."

"Ha, ha, I get it! You're getting your own back for my little joke about the envelope," I said, laughing loudly and slapping my thighs, before lifting my hands and reaching over to take her in my arms. When she raised her fist I arrested my forward motion and covered my face, just in case, and when I peeped through my fingers she was preparing to leave.

"Go to the Laguna Beach campsite and wait for further instructions," she said, in her businesslike tone once more.

"Do I have to stay put all the time?"

"No, just in the mornings. After one o'clock you can do as you please. I'm not promising anything though, so don't get your hopes up."

"But can I count on you to put a good word in for me?"

She sighed. "I suppose so. I'd rather work with you than some of the other fools I've had to deal with."

"What happened to them? Sacked, I suppose."

"One sacked, two in prison and one disappeared after a rendezvous with… that man."

I laughed and made an oinking sound. "Fed to the pigs, eh?"

"You really are unbelievable, Geoff."

"I know. I shall count the days till I see you again, my sweetness and light."

"Hasta luego," she said curtly, and was gone.

5

Laguna Beach campsite was fairly similar to the nudist one, except that people wore clothes. Funnily enough, whenever I hit the pool or beach and saw a ravishing babe my blood *did* flow towards my main erogenous zone, which was inconvenient but also a relief, as I'd feared that the time I'd spent subduing my animal instincts might have begun to emasculate me. Though I never missed an opportunity to chat to any acceptably attractive ladies at the new site, their reactions to my gallant advances were so cool that I began to think there might be something in Claudia's jest regarding a strong lesbic presence in the area. No other explanation occurred to me, so when a buxom young wench did deign to respond to my attempt to pass the time of day – but refused a dinner invitation on the grounds that she had a previous engagement with her slender young friend, Esme, who she pointed out across the pool – I put my hands on my hips, smiled knowingly and told her that I'd be delighted to invite the pair of them to a first-class nosh-up in town.

"Well, that's very kind of you, but we've already made arrangements," she said, looking down and slapping the water from her colossal thighs. She was more Harry's cup of tea really, but I'm not averse to giving away a bit of weight in the sack from time to time, as variety is the spice of life. She then looked so longingly at her svelte friend that any remaining doubts I had about her orientation were instantly erased.

"How about tomorrow night, Chelo?" I said, for that was her name.

"Er, I'll ask Esme later and let you know tomorrow, if that's all right."

"Fine, just fine. A few drinks, a bite to eat, then I'll show you Bambi."

"Who's Bambi?" she asked, her chins folding in perplexity.

"Bambi's my van. Look, you can just see her through the trees."

"That? Is it a real van?"

"Yep, she's small, but her suspension's rock solid, if you know what I mean," I said with a wink, for I've never been one to beat about the bush for too long and I saw little point in wining and dining them, only to be ditched after such an expense.

"I must go now," she said after scanning me feverishly from top to toe.

"Bambi's got two beds, so we'll have to use our imagination," I said, gyrating my hips and doing a Michael Jackson-style move without actually laying hands on my tackle, as it was a family site. When she glowered and raised her ham-like arm I feared momentarily for my still bruised nose, so when she turning and dived into the water, creating a minor tidal wave, I didn't feel too dejected, as it had been a longshot all along.

Imagine my surprise when I saw them later on, both hand in hand with a pair of skinny young lads, who I can only assume had a larger camper van than me. After that minor debacle I decided to keep myself to myself and just wait for Miss Right, or Miss Not Too Bad, to come along, and I was still waiting five days later when to my immense delight Claudia arrived while I was reading a copy of *Fifty Shades of Grey* that I'd found in the loo. I don't normally read such trash, preferring serious authors like Terry Pratchett, J.K. Rowling, and George R.R. Martin, so I chucked the filthy thing under Bambi and stood to greet her.

"At last, love of my life," I said, holding out both hands.

She was wearing, from her feet up, white canvas shoes, blue denim shorts, a black Joaquín Sabina t-shirt and a straw hat that would have looked silly on anyone else, but not on Claudia, or possibly me, but rather than grasping the proffered hands she walked straight into the back of Bambi, so I joined her there and closed the door.

"Open it," she said, before lighting a cigarette.

I did as requested and sat down opposite her. "Er, I don't normally like people smoking in here, dear."

"Why not? It still stinks and the floor's filthy."

I jumped up and quickly binned a couple of snotty kitchen towels, before opening my side window. When I began to straddle her to open the other, she pushed me playfully back onto my bench.

"So, you're a Joaquín Sabina fan, are you?" I asked, pointing at the sketchy likeness of that famous Spanish singer-songwriter.

"Yes, I love his songs. Right, you–"

"I almost met him once," I said, being in no hurry to get down to business, as I wished to maximise my time with my gorgeous colleague, not least because I wanted the frigid campsite totty to see who *did* penetrate into Bambi's innards.

"What do you mean, almost?"

"He's from Úbeda, near Jaén."

"I know."

"I was there once with my sweetheart at the time, Carmela, a great beauty like you."

"And?"

"Well, we were in a bar and I got chatting to a policeman," I said, having decided to build up the suspense little by little.

She frowned. "Hmm, you seem to like cops."

"This one was called Curro. That's short for Francisco."

"I *know* that. I'm not a bloody foreigner like you."

"He told me that his father had also been a policeman."

"Whoopee," she said, or words to that effect.

"Think about what I'm saying, Claudia."

"Can you get to the point, Geoff? I can't stay here long."

"OK, which famous... person's father and brother are policemen?"

"How the hell should I know? Are you drunk?" she said, sniffing the air.

"You're not on the ball today, love. Which famous singer-songwriter's father and brother are both policemen?"

"Oh, wasn't Sabina's dad a cop? I remember reading that he got him out of trouble once."

"Yes, and his brother's a cop too. It was his *brother* I spoke to in that bar in Úbeda back in.... oh, a long time ago."

"Really?" she said, sitting up straighter on realising the full weight of my statement.

"Yes, we spent quite a while chatting away," I said, glancing out of the window, pursing my lips and nodding slowly.

"Right, so did he introduce you to Joaquín or something?"

"Not exactly."

"What then?"

"Well, he said that his brother occasionally visited Úbeda to see the family. I asked him if we'd be able to meet him the next time he came, as Carmela was a huge fan." I stroked my still slightly tender nose.

"And did you?"

"What?"

"Meet him?"

"No, when I said that he finished his coffee and said he had to hurry – he was on duty, you see – but he did shake my hand."

Claudia's head fell and she covered it with her cellist's hands, before rocking slowly to and fro.

"So, you see, I actually *shook* Sabina's brother's hand."

She grunted.

"Exactly the same genetic make-up, you know, give or take a chromosome or two."

She raised her head and looked at me with doe-like eyes. "I wish I'd never worn this bloody t-shirt now."

"I can play you a couple of Sabina songs if you like," I said, jumping up to retrieve my guitar from the space over the cab. "*Princesa*? *Calle Melancolía*?"

"No, no thanks."

"All right, another time then," I said, relieved because I wasn't altogether sure of the chords, or the words.

"Right, if you've finally finished talking crap, I'll tell you what Hugo wants you to do for him."

"Is he back?"

"Yes."

"Let's drive over then. I haven't seen him for ages."

"He isn't especially keen to clap eyes on you, though he did believe me when I said you were sorry about your tremendous cock-up. Besides, we don't *do* social calls. We keep contact to a minimum, for obvious reasons."

"But aren't you living there?"

"Of course not. I was just looking after the house."

I leant to one side – my left, I think – and propped my head on my hand. "So where do you live, honey?"

"That, you will never, ever know, Geoff."

"Ha, they all say that. So what's the plan?"

"Well, Hugo thinks it best for you to have as little to do with people as possible, so you won't be transporting any more, despite it being the high season for, er… tourism now."

"Right, well, I don't mind that, as I'm not altogether happy about the ethical aspects of people… carrying."

"If we don't do it, somebody else will."

"If you say so," I said smugly, though I had to admit that she had a point. "What am I to transport then, chocolate truffles?"

Her response to my witty riposte was surprising, as her lovely eyes opened wide, then narrowed sharply, before she scrunched them closed, after which they resumed their standard aperture.

"Something wrong, Claudia?"

"No, no. Er, what made you say what you just said?"

"About what?"

"About chocolate something-or-other."

"Truffles?"

"Yes."

"Oh, just irony, as I'm sure Hugo will have something more valuable for me to shift."

"Right," she said, wiping her moist brow.

"Besides, they'd melt. Chocolate ones, I mean."

She then startled me by dropping to her knees and gripping my thighs. So, I thought, she *is* made of flesh and blood after all. As her head began to fall I gently held the tip of her chin and looked into her eyes.

"A little kissing first, I think," I said.

"*Why* did you mention truffles, Geoff?" she said in a quavering voice. "Nobody knows about them except Hugo and me."

"Now, now," I said, moving my lips towards hers, upon which she pushed herself up and began to caress my neck. "Gently, dear," I added, as her ardour was making breathing difficult. Then she surprised me yet again by releasing me, slumping back on the other bed, falling to one side and bursting into tears. I gently closed the door, as this was the last thing I wished the jealous campsite ladies to see, and when her sobs had subsided to a whimper I sat down beside her and stroked her hair.

"Claudia, dear, do you want to tell me what's wrong?" I said, before deftly whipping a clean kitchen towel from my shorts and placing it around her divine little nose. "Blow," I said.

She blew, before taking the towel, wiping her eyes with the snotless edges and sitting up. "I just can't work you out, Geoff."

"I've often been called an enigma, among other things."

"I can't decide if you're incredibly stupid or astoundingly shrewd."

"Take your pick, babe," I said with a chuckle, glad that she was feeling better. Time of the month, I guessed, as it often makes women prone to odd behaviour, but at least she'd shown her hitherto well-concealed sensitivity and we were finally making progress.

"How on earth did you know about the truffles?"

"Oh, just a logical deduction," I said, though I hadn't a clue what she was on about.

"How?"

"I can't explain it. I suppose it's a sort of sixth sense. I just sniff things out, including truffles." I chuckled and took her hand, which she allowed me to hold for a while, before she suddenly stiffened.

"There, there. Shall we just lie down for a while?"

Rather than comply, she shook my hand off, leapt for her bag and pulled out a small handgun, which she then pointed at me.

"Er, Claudia, that sort of thing doesn't really turn me on, you know. A little light spanking, maybe, but not guns. They're liable to go off, though I don't suppose it's loaded."

"It is loaded. I've just realised that there can only be one explanation for your… knowledge," she said, keeping the piece aimed at my chest, a hard target to miss.

"Fire away. No! I mean, tell me."

"You must be working for that bastard Axel. You've infiltrated our outfit by pretending to be the dumbest guy who ever lived."

My first instinct was to string her along for a while longer, but in view of the pressure her finger was exerting on the trigger I thought this unwise.

I cleared my rather dry throat. "Claudia, Harry met Laura in Las Negras on the Cabo de Gata. We then visited her house in Canillas on our way to Gibraltar. I mentioned that I was looking for work and she called Hugo to see if he had anything for me. I visited Hugo and then we continued our journey. Then I came back, went to Hugo's house and met your lovely self. That's all there is to it."

"But… the truffles?"

"I just happened to say truffles. I might have chosen another type of confectionary or another insignificant item. Maybe you don't understand English humour. Now please put that thing down or I'm going to pee my pants."

She lowered the gun, sat down and gazed fixedly at me. "I'm just going to have to believe you."

"That's my girl."

"If you *are* in with Axel I'm finished anyway, so I might as well believe you."

"There you are then. Now, what's all this fuss about truffles? I don't even like the damn things."

"If I tell you I'll dig an even deeper pit for myself," she mumbled.

"What does it matter? If, like you said, I'm in with Axel, you're a dead duck, so you might as well spit it out."

"Hugo's planning to muscle in on Axel's truffle trade. There, I've said it." She placed the dainty pistol back in her handbag and snapped it shut.

"Ha, ha, ha," I began, before continuing to laugh for some time, until I saw that my gaiety wasn't putting her at her ease, as intended, but making her reach for her bag once more. I shut my mouth and dried my eyes. "But Claudia, who on earth wants to smuggle truffles? Why, you can buy a box in a supermarket for a few euros."

She pushed her bag away. "You really haven't got a bloody clue about truffles, have you?"

"I know that in a mixed box of chocolates they're the ones I leave till last, apart from maybe Turkish Delight, though I blow hot and cold with them. I like them with coffee, but not with tea. It's funny that, isn't it?"

Though she didn't answer, she must have agreed, for a moment later *she* was rolling about on the bed, convulsed with laughter. This really was turning into one of the most surprising mornings of my life and as it was getting rather stuffy in there I opened the door, keen to show any passing babes what a good time was to be had in Bambi. When she had ceased to hoot and writhe I handed her another clean kitchen towel and patiently waited for an explanation.

She staggered to the door and pulled it shut, before sitting down directly opposite me. "Geoff, forget chocolate truffles. I'm talking about real truffles. Truffles that come out of the ground."

"The ones that pigs sniff out?"

"Yes, though they use dogs nowadays as the pigs tend to eat them. The best truffles are the white ones that are found in northern Italy. They sell for huge prices all over the world and Hugo wishes to sell them to the top Spanish restaurants."

"So are they more expensive than the chocolate ones? I once bought a box from Marks and Spencer for a cute chick and they cost me over a tenner."

"A kilo of white Alba truffles can sell for €5,000, sometimes more if the season has been dry."

"Right, yes, that's quite a lot. Are they illegal?"

"No, they're food."

"Then why don't the restaurants just order them through the usual channels?"

"They do, but there's a little thing called tax that many restaurateurs don't wish to pay. After Italian tax and Spanish tax the price is prohibitive, so Hugo has sourced an illicit supplier."

"The same one as Axel?"

"No, Axel is a vicious, merciless brute, but Hugo is by far the better businessman. As soon as the first white truffles are available, hopefully in September, he intends to speed them to restaurants all over Spain. That way he'll establish himself as their supplier for the rest of the autumn and winter."

"Nothing doing in summer then?"

"Italian summer truffles are not so special. There are plenty of Spanish truffles to satisfy the summer market. In September we will be ready and, God willing, will outstrip the competition."

"Are you very religious, Claudia?" I asked, hoping that this wouldn't be yet another obstacle to us becoming bedfellows.

"Where white truffles are concerned, yes. Cars, tobacco, people and… other things are all very well, but it's in the truffle market that we can make a big impact. Lateral thinking, Hugo calls it. Finding a niche market and exploiting it thoroughly."

"He sounds like Alan Sugar."

"Who's that?"

"Never mind, you wouldn't like him. So, let me guess. I'm to drive Bambi round the coast to Italy and wait for the first load of truffles. Then I'm to hurtle back through France and get that... er, truffly gold to the restaurants double-quick."

"Don't be preposterous, Geoff. You'd have to pass through two customs posts and the truffles would be a sticky, inedible mess by the time you got to your destination." She shook her hair back and laughed merrily, looking like her old self again.

"I'm glad I amuse you," I said, also amused.

"Oh, you do, Geoff, and I'm now convinced that you've had nothing to do with Axel. How could you? You'd be dead by now."

"The only Axel I know is Axel Merckx, son of Eddy, the greatest racing cyclist who ever lived, and also a cyclist. I almost met Eddy once. I was in Ostend one day with a pretty–"

"Never mind, tell me another day."

I clicked my fingers. "Why don't we fly the truffles back?"

"Because at airports one has to go through customs."

"Good point."

"If things go well Hugo will charter private aircraft, but at first we must rely on a flawless transport chain with several links. The truffles will reach a certain point on the Spanish shore by high-speed boat, where driver A will pick them up and take them to a certain city. Drivers B, C, D, and E will then split the load and distribute it around Spain. Speed will be of the essence, especially at first when the weather is still hot, as truffles don't keep very well, but oughtn't to be frozen. They can be refrigerated, but must be allowed to breathe, so we are considering the simple solution of large blocks of ice."

"Sounds good. Where do I fit in?"

Claudia opened her mouth to speak, but then clamped it shut and covered her face with her hands. "I don't know. I don't know why the hell I'm telling you all this. *How* is it that you make me babble on like a stupid little girl?"

"A knack, but don't worry, mum's the word for now, eh?"

"Definitely, or I'll be out of a job."

"I'm a tomb."

"Good. Now I'll have to convince Hugo to make you one of the drivers, probably driver A, as he'll travel the shortest distance and this stupid crate must be dead slow."

"She once hit fifty-nine miles per hour; that's almost a ton in kilometres," I said, recalling Jeremy's daring descent to the coast.

"Pathetic, *but*, on the other hand, it's vitally important that the beach pick-up be made in a vehicle that no self-respecting smuggler would use and that the police wouldn't suspect for an instant, driven by a person who looks more like a clueless *guiri* tourist than a criminal," she said, *guiri* being an affectionate word for foreigner.

"Your eloquence amazes me, Claudia."

"Just rehearsing what I'll say to Hugo. Yes, I think I'll be able to convince him, *if* you don't bungle your next task."

"Bring it on, babe."

"It's a simple job, and quite appropriate really, as it will be similar to your work on Project T."

"What's that when it's at home?"

"The project we've just been discussing and which you are to erase from your mind until further notice."

"Ah, I get it. T for truffles," I said, the word for truffle in Spanish being *trufa*.

She sighed. "Yes, now forget them. Right, next Wednesday you are to drive down to a place which I will signal on this map," she said, extracting a photocopied map from her handbag.

"OK, just leave it with me."

"No, Geoff, you must memorise the place. Don't worry, it's not difficult. So, there the procedure will be similar to last time. You will leave the van for an hour with the key under the mat."

"Hey, will it be the same guys as last time?"

"That is no concern of yours, and you *won't* be seeing them, will you?"

"Course not. I still sometimes wonder where those lads were from."

"Well don't, because you know that curiosity killed the cat," she said, the expression being the same in Spanish, as my translations are and will continue to be as near to the original as humanly possible.

"OK, sugarpie. What next?"

"From there you will drive to a city a little under two hundred kilometres away, where you will–"

"Let me guess. I leave Bambi with the key under the mat and clear off."

"You're a fast learner, Geoff."

"Thanks. So, what's the route?"

"I'll come to that in a moment. First I must tell you that though the job is straightforward, the cargo is of a slightly sensitive nature and if you are caught you may be sent to prison for a... while. On the plus side, your remuneration will be suitably high. Hugo wishes me to tell you this and if you still agree to do the job to then give you the details."

"Not drugs?"

"I've already told you that we don't do drugs."

"Not people?"

"I've already told you that you will never transport people again."

"Check."

"What?"

"OK. Right, if it's not drugs or people it can't be that bad, so I'll do it."

"Are you sure?"

"Sure I'm sure."

Claudia had been behaving quite rationally for quite a while by then, so when she stood up and began to move her head in circles I feared that another mood swing was on the way.

"You OK, honey? Can I get you a beer or something?"

"Are they cold?" she said, now moving her head from side to side and breathing deeply.

"Of course. Bambi's got all the mod cons," I said, fishing a couple of cans of *Mahou* lager from the tiny fridge and handing her one.

She then concluded her calisthenics, sat down, opened the beer and took a sip. I did likewise and awaited my instructions.

"Geoff, knowing you as I do, I *know* you'll want to know what you're carrying and I *know* you'll probably stop to take a look at some point, so, to remove this temptation I'm going to go against Hugo's strict instructions and tell you what it is. God knows, I've blabbed enough already today, so a little more can't do any harm."

"As you wish, Claudia, though I assure you I wouldn't have looked. Last time I was a rookie, but now I'm a seasoned professional, but tell me anyway as I'm a man you can trust," I said, partly to reassure her and partly because I liked the sound of the words.

"Right, you'll be transporting arms."

"Human arms?" I blurted out, as I'd just been scratching my right one.

"No, you idiot, guns and things."

"That's what I meant. Arms used by humans," I said, keen to conceal my gaffe. "Ammo too?" I added coolly.

"Good God, no, not in this heap."

I narrowed my eyes and gave her a steely squint. "Hey, who are these arms for? Not bad people, I hope?"

"No, no, they're… not for bad people. They're for… well, in the city in question the local police force are jealous of the national police and the civil guard, as they've got much better guns than them, so they've ordered a few new weapons, but need to get them secretly so there'll be no fuss."

"I understand," I said, though she hadn't taken me in for a moment. In any case, guns are only harmful if people pull the triggers, which is a personal decision at the end of the day. In the USA people are allowed to own guns and they all seem happy about that, so why shouldn't a law-abiding Spaniard not be able to keep a small revolver, like Claudia's, on their bedside table?

"Are you sure, Geoff? When I give you the itinerary you can't go back on your word."

"As if."

"What?"

"I won't, scout's honour."

She unfolded the map. "Right, look, you will drive along the coast to a village called Maro, just past Nerja. You will drive down to the beach. There's only one, but it's quite a way away, so have a good look at this lane here."

I looked and took a mental photograph. "Got it."

"Right, you will reach the end of the lane at 0300 hours next Wednesday. That's three o'clock in the morning."

"I *know* that, honeybun."

"You will turn the van around and leave it in a parking place as near to the beach as possible. You will get yourself off the lane and walk cross-country for ten minutes. Then you will conceal yourself in the undergrowth – behind a bush, or something – for forty minutes, before returning to the van."

"Shall I take a torch?"

"No, it's a full moon that night."

"How do you know?"

"I just do."

"What if it's cloudy?"

"Highly unlikely. If it is you'll just have to manage."

"Fair enough. Ha, I'll eat plenty of carrots before then, but wouldn't it be easier to do it in daylight? Less suspicious, you know."

"In July I imagine the beach will be full of people during the day, Geoff."

"Good point. So, at about 0400 hours I head off from there. Where to?"

"You will drive eastwards along the coast as far as Motril."

"I know it."

"Then you will drive north past Granada."

"I know it."

"You will continue north and approximately one hour later you will reach your destination."

"Great. Where's that then?"

"You know the place. You mentioned it earlier."

"Refresh my memory, babe."

"The city of Jaén."

I gulped. "Jaén?"

"Jaén." Her eyes bored into mine. "Any problem?"

"No, no, no," I said, a vision of Carmela as she was then swimming across my mind's eye. Swimming because she was swimming, in the municipal pool, where we often went to while away the sultry summer afternoons.

"You seem worried. You've been chosen for the Jaén run because you told me that you lived there for several years. You will drive to the Peñamefécit part of the city."

"The Peña-what-what-what part of the city?"

"Peñamefécit. Don't you know it?"

"It rings a bell," I lied, as during my time there I'd stuck pretty much to the centre, having rented a small apartment near the cathedral and not too far from the language school.

She sighed, opened her bag and extracted two more photocopied sheets. "Here is a plan of the city, showing where Peñamefécit is."

"Ah, yes, I remember now."

"And here is a more detailed plan. At exactly 0700 hours you will park outside this bakery on this street."

"Then I leave the key under the mat and clear off for an hour."

"No."

"No?"

"No, you return exactly twelve hours later, at 1900 hours, as our contacts have requested a longer period to effect the handover."

"To the local police station, eh?"

"Wherever they wish. On returning to the van you will find a single envelope under the left-hand bed. This is for you, as Hugo's payment will reach him by other channels. You'll be glad of the extra time, as you'll be able to revisit the city of your youth."

"Yes," I said, gulping again, as with all the talk of this Peñamefécit place I'd forgotten I was going to Jaén, home of the beauty I'd loved and left, and her rather primitive brothers. I sipped my beer and smiled, the promise of a big payday outweighing a niggling fear that one or more of those brothers might spot me and exact their revenge for my – it has to be said – rather shoddy treatment of their delectable sister. It had happened over twenty years ago, but as I had scarcely aged at all I'd have to keep a low profile, lest they nab me and submit me to an Axel-style fate, as they too owned sundry livestock, not to mention lots of shotguns, animal traps and the like. Still, I reflected as I sipped away under Claudia's relentless gaze, Jaén was a pretty big place and if I kept my head down I ought to get through the day undetected.

"Have you memorised the plan yet?" she asked.

"What? Oh, I might need a bit more time for that. There are an awful lot of streets."

"Hmm, keep this one for now then, but you mustn't take it with you on the day."

"The night," I corrected.

"Yes, the night. So, next Wednesday, eight days from now." She smiled and gazed into my ardent eyes. "Can I count on you, Geoff?"

"Of course. It's a cinch."

"Repeat the instructions to me."

I did so, flawlessly, and she purred with contentment.

"My head's on the line with this one, Geoff. If anything goes wrong I'll be for the chop, and so will you."

I chuckled and patted her knee. "Figuratively speaking, of course."

She frowned. "Don't mess up."

"I won't, and after this we'll be snuffling truffles all winter long, eh?"

"*Don't* mention truffles. Don't even think about them."

"OK, mum's the word," I said with a playful snort, and before I could grasp her hands to give them a farewell squeeze she was up and out of Bambi like a lithe little lynx, which was the animal she most reminded me of, barring the fangs, though her upper canines were quite well developed.

After she had gone I paced up and down inside Bambi, a rather restricted activity but excellent for concentrating the mind. I congratulated myself on the successful outcome of our sometimes fraught encounter – for it really had seemed for a moment like Hugo might be handing me the old P45 – and it was only after fifty or sixty laps of the van that I juddered to a halt, threw my hands to my head, sank down onto the left-hand bed and broke out in a cold sweat. Claudia, my own sweet Claudia, had pointed a *gun* at me!

Not only that, but, as I said at the time, her finger had been very much on the trigger and I'd practically seen the muscles, if fingers have muscles, tensing that vile appendage. Not only did this realisation make my all too short life flash before my eyes, but it also caused me to review my whole attitude to gun ownership, as if Claudia really was at the business end of her menstrual cycle my life had just been hanging by the finest of threads, rather like the… never mind.

Having begun to get used to these cold sweats by now, I just sat with my head in my hands until the worst was over, before reaching for the rapidly shrinking kitchen roll and yanking off a couple of sheets. No sooner had I dried my clammy forehead and composed myself than *another* cold sweat broke out, this time due to the sudden recollection of my destination on Wednesday week. Jaén! Carmela! Her sinister siblings! A Bambiful of guns! Once again I let my unruly glands do their worst and after this second secretion I felt much better; purged, one might say, of my irrational fears. I chuckled to myself before itemising the true state of affairs:

Claudia would never have pulled the trigger.
Carmela's brothers will never spot me.
The guns are (probably) for those valiant boys in blue.
I'm going to get paid tons of money.

Pleased with these logical deductions, I decided to write them down on the back of the street plan, so that I could take a peek if I suffered another attack of the collywobbles. This done, I grabbed my towel and went for a well-deserved swim in the pool, not forgetting to shower first, and resolved to put my forthcoming mission out of my mind.

6

A week later – my ability to compartmentalise my life having enabled me to switch off, chill out and give scarcely a thought to the impending operation – after checking Bambi's roadworthiness down to the last detail I left the campsite where I'd frolicked like a spring lamb day in and day out – coming ever to close to seducing a ravishing young Norwegian chick – and headed along the coast to Nerja.

Now, if Harry were to read this account up to press, two things would occur to him. One, or A, he would have to admit that my facility with words is second to none and that the account of our holiday ought – with all due respect to Jeremy – have been written by me; and two, or B, that his young pal Geoff will undoubtedly screw up his next assignment, because deep down he's a bit of a buffoon and just isn't cut out for an undertaking that would scare the pants off most of my (i.e. his) erstwhile colleagues, myself (himself) included. Harry may never read any of this, as it might not be prudent to publish it during what remains of his life, but loath as I am to disappoint him, and any other sceptics out there, I'm happy to say that the *Maro-Jaén Gun Run* went off without a hitch, as I knew it would.

In fact it was such a humdrum sort of outing that I'm in two minds whether or not to bother writing about it, but I suppose I ought to fill you in on a routine night and day in the life of a freelance smuggler, as although Hugo was technically my employer I was beginning to feel very much in the driver's seat, figuratively as well as actually, and I knew that sooner rather than later I'd be casting off my Belgian yoke and going it alone. Anyway, after filling Bambi's tank I had a bite to eat and killed some time in a roadside pub, before driving the last couple of miles to Maro and trundling down the lane to the beach, reaching the end of it at 0258 hours. The moon was indeed full, as scheduled, so after executing a rapid five-point turn in the lane I left Bambi facing the village, about half a mile away, and slipped the key under the mat, before hopping over a steel safety barrier and heading into the undergrowth. Claudia hadn't specified in which direction I must spend ten minutes walking, nor at what speed, so I ambled westward through the prickly scrub and, lo and behold, after exactly ten minutes I still had an excellent view of the short, sandy beach which lay a further couple of hundred yards below Bambi down a narrow concrete track.

As soon as I'd stretched out on the dusty earth I heard the sound of an engine and made out a shadowy craft approaching the beach. The engine cut out and before I could say or think Jack Robinson, or maybe Jack Ronald Reginald Robinson, I saw three spectral figures tramping up the beach laden with rucksacks. They disappeared from view, but a few minutes later they reappeared and snatched fresh sacks from the two ghostly beings on the beach – making five commandoes in all, six if you include me – which they lugged from the shoreline while I silently urged them on. So, with six heavy sacks in the back of Bambi I expected them to cast off after their second trip, but to my immense surprise my catlike eyes witnessed the three of them getting to grips with a long, heavy package which they manfully conveyed up the beach, straining under the weight of an item which I couldn't for the life of me imagine what purpose it might have for the local police force. Maybe they'd ordered a mammoth bazooka or a compact anti-tank gun for strictly ceremonial use, but it wasn't for me to reason why, so after watching the boat – a dinghy, I think – roar off into the placid Med I counted to a hundred very slowly before leaping up, dusting myself down and hotfooting it back to Bambi, tripping up twice in my haste to get my part of the show on the road.

I set off a bit sooner than scheduled, but the truth is that the quasi-military manoeuvres I'd been privileged to observe had got the old adrenaline flowing, so I simply couldn't hold myself back. Bambi, on the other hand, was in no hurry to begin our vital leg of the journey, as when I pressed on the accelerator she refused to budge, she being parked on an especially steep section of the lane. Thinking on my feet, I released the handbrake and allowed her to drift slowly back to a slightly flatter bit, whereupon I applied her brakes, causing her to test my patience by beginning to skid alarmingly, a slide only arrested by the concrete buffers strategically placed to prevent careless motorists from plunging down a precipice. As well as a dull crunch there was also a tinkling of glass, and as far as I know if one were to visit Maro Beach even today, one may still find the mangled and shattered information board that helped to cushion the blow on that starry night, though they might have got round to changing it by now.

After inspecting the damage, not insignificant due to the absence of a rear bumper, I checked that the rear door would still open, which it did, and on viewing the sinister mass of hardware within I was sorely tempted to grab my torch and have a shufty, but at that moment headlights appeared further up the lane, so I slammed the door and dived back into the cab, where I hunkered down until the vehicle had passed. Alas, it couldn't pass, as we were at the end of the lane, so when the hatchback eased into a space only five yards away – young lovers, no doubt – I started her up and hit the gas sufficiently hard for Bambi to plough up the rise and leave the scene, without, I might add, turning on the lights, as the last thing I wanted was for the canoodling couple to see an easily memorisable British number plate. Pleased with my quick thinking in the face of adversity I eventually engaged second gear, flicked on the lights and soon reached the village.

On the undulating coast road east I found Bambi's handling to be unprecedentedly heavy, but only when I joined the motorway a few wobbly miles later did I realise the full extent of her bellicose burden. Harry, as you know, is a large fat man – technically obese, I should think – and while Jeremy and I are of more modest proportions, with the three of us on board, plus all our luggage, Bambi had just about as much as she could handle on our often arduous route through Spain. This load, however, was something else, as try as I might I could not persuade her to exceed forty mph, except on the all too brief downhills, so although the traffic was light at that time of night, I couldn't help feeling a tad conspicuous and rather hoped I wouldn't come across a patrol car containing two restless cops.

On heading north after passing Motril those restful descents became a thing of the past as the road climbed steadily towards Granada, and as I urged my plucky little van onwards and upwards – sometimes cajoling, sometimes yelling – it dawned on me that I might not make my 0700 hours deadline, but short of leaving a pile of weapons by the roadside there wasn't much I could do about it. So, as it wasn't my fault I ceased to fret and when I finally pulled up outside the bakery in Peñamefécit at 0757 hours I simply concealed the key and sauntered away from that surprisingly multi-ethnic part of town.

All that remained was to evade detection by any or all of Carmela's three brothers; one a farmer with a penchant for guns – he would have loved to see my load – another a builder and part-time farmer with a penchant for hunting, and the third a butcher and pig breeder with a penchant for battle re-enactments, preferably with live ammunition. In the intervening years they might have become Buddhists or Quakers for all I knew, but I doubted it, so I took the precaution of donning a baseball cap, sunglasses and a red cotton scarf which covered my nose and mouth. The Spanish, generally speaking, are softies when it comes to cold weather and in winter are often to be seen with a similar garment, worn – futilely, I think – to ward off colds and flu. As it was late July and the temperature was pushing thirty-five degrees this preventative purpose wasn't credible, so I decided to feign illness and explain, if asked, that my covering was a means of protecting bystanders from contamination.

This entailed a lot of coughing, spluttering and apologetic eye rolling, and after a couple of hours spent touring the city centre I became heartily sick of being the centre of attention, as all eyes seemed to be upon me as I shuffled and sneezed my way from place to place. In the splendid cathedral a priest asked me if I was mortally ill and on my responding that I had a touch of pneumonia he suggested that I light a few electric candles and pray for my soul. As the aged cleric continued to hover around, I did so, and after praying for a good payday I left that holy edifice and strolled over to the *Baños Arabes*, or Arab Baths, the oldest and largest that are open to the public in Europe, but was refused admission due to my garb and distressing state, as it's a fact that when one fakes ill health genuine symptoms usually follow, which explained my profuse sweating and haggard appearance, though I must say it's a bit thick not to let a chap with a scarf over his face enter a Muslim bathhouse.

A while later I found myself unable to resist entering a small bar which I used to frequent with Carmela, and I was relieved to see an unknown young man behind the bar, so after apologising for my poor health I ordered a beer, before repairing to the corner table where the two of us used to sip wine and whisper sweet nothings in those heady days of my youth, until Carmela became just too clinging and I was forced to beat a retreat back to Blighty. Imagine my surprise when a stout, aproned lady emerged from the kitchen and stood staring fixedly at me. When she began to waddle towards me I attempted a spot of whooping cough to ward her off, for her face rang a bell, but to no avail, as a moment later her stout legs were planted before me, her lardy arms folded, and her beady eyes staring into my sunglasses.

"Why, if it isn't Chef!" she cried, Chef being how the local people had pronounced my name.

"Cough, cough, whoop, cough," I went on. "Who?" I added, before pulling down the scarf that I'd lifted to imbibe my beer.

"Oh, Chef, I'd recognise those knobbly knees anywhere. You do look ill though. You shouldn't be wearing shorts and drinking cold beer," she said, whisking it from under my nose. "I'll prepare you a bowl of broth," she added, before turning and lumbering back into the kitchen.

I could have cleared off right away, of course, but seeing Marta again, twenty-odd years on and sixty pounds heavier, made me cast off my disguise, as we'd been great pals back in the day, when she'd been quite a stunner and had I not chosen Carmela she might have been the lucky one. When she returned with the broth she remarked on my miraculous recovery, before going to fetch a bottle of local wine and two glasses.

"Ah, Chef, you always were a great joker, but why that ridiculous disguise?"

"Er, well, to be honest I had to come here on business and I was a bit worried about bumping into Carmela's brothers."

"Pablo, Paco and Pepe? But they would be delighted to see you, I'm sure. In fact, I think I have Paco's number in my little book. Would you like to call him? Or will you pop into the butcher's?"

Marta, I realised, was far from being *au fait* with Carmela's brothers' sanguinary attitude towards me, so rather than filling her in on the threats that the three men would undoubtedly have made had they seen me before I departed under cover of night, I told her that I would indeed be dropping by the shop during the course of the day.

"Do that, he'll be delighted."

"No doubt," I replied, picturing his fierce face and the array of knives at his disposal.

"So what kind of business are you involved in now, Chef?"

"It's… just a moment. I must visit the bathroom, then I'll tell you."

"Very well, I'll bring us something more to eat."

In the sanctuary of the cubicle I pulled down my shorts, merely to aid thought as I didn't need to 'go', and racked my brains for a suitable response to Marta's question. I could have told her any old thing, of course, but conscious of the fact that Harry would soon be calling me and inviting me up to Canillas to see him and his Belgian beloved, I decided that it was as good a time as any to think on my feet, or my bottom, and come up with a viable and easily demonstrable occupation for myself. My mind is at its keenest when under pressure, and as I knew that my mobile could ring any day now I wished to be able to respond instantly to Harry's probably probing questions, as if he detected the slightest hint of deception he'd soon be prying and piss-taking as only he knows how. On emerging from the cubicle, after flushing the empty loo, I had a provisional plan which I would test out on Marta, so I returned to the bar all smiles, as our chance encounter was proving useful after all.

"It's so nice to see you after all this time, Marta. I'm glad I called in now," I said as I seated myself.

"It's good to see you too. It was such a shame that you had to leave here under a cloud, as I for one never believed that you really fondled that girl's bottom in class and I defended you for many days, until everybody forgot about you. She was a terrible strumpet, and how were you to know she was only fifteen?"

"I don't recall that incident very well, Marta," I said, which was true, as although I believe some such nonsense got back to the owner of the language school, that purely accidental pat – I'd been reaching for my chalk – had nothing whatsoever to do with my midnight flit. As you see, I hold nothing back in this candid account, not even a scatterbrained matron's ramblings, but before she could reminisce further about that misunderstanding I told her how I was keeping the wolf from the door.

"I sell fireworks now, Marta?"

"Fireworks?"

"Yes, I tour the whole of Andalucía, selling from my van."

"Who buys them? If one wants fireworks, one can go to a shop or buy them online."

I held up a forefinger and waggled it to and fro. "Ah, yes, but in the villages there are no shops and… and the internet connection is sometimes poor. I arrive there, display my wares and people take the opportunity to stock up for the local fiestas, or just to have some handy in case they fancy letting a few off," I said, and as I looked into her eyes I imagined Harry's bottomless brown pools gazing back at me.

Before I go on I ought to tell you by what logical process I decided on fireworks while ruminating in the cubicle, and the truth is that it was a series of interlinking brainwaves which made me choose that particular product, initiated by the discovery of the wrapper from a *traca*, or string of firecrackers, at my feet. On running that type of merchandise past myself I discovered that it met all my requirements for an affordable, portable and sellable product which was a little out of the ordinary. I mean, I could simply stock up on clothes or shoes and tell Harry that I peddled them at markets, but that would be so predictable and mundane that he would immediately set about chaffing me for my lack of imagination. No, it had to be something that would explain why I had shelved Hugo's offer of work, and as people don't know much about fireworks I could, after a little research, blind them with pyrotechnical science and convince them that I was onto a winner. *Them*, I say, because Laura too would be all ears, and by telling her that Hugo and I were yet to work together I hoped to bring out her true colours and enable me to ascertain just how much she knew about her Belgian buddy's dubious business activities.

I apologise if this is a lot to take in, especially in the middle of my conversation with Marta, but by relating my quick-fire thought processes in this way I hope the reader will become aware of how a brain like mine works. As Albert Einstein once said, 'The true sign of intelligence is not knowledge but imagination,' but let's get back to Marta.

"Well, Chef, that sounds all right, but to be honest I expected something better of you. Though the classroom was clearly no place for you, I imagined you would prosper back in your own country, where I'm sure people understand you better."

"Oh, I've worked as an employment adviser and a hotel manager since then, and also run bars and sold motorcycles, but what is money if one cannot enjoy it?"

"What indeed?" she said, wide-eyed with admiration.

"I simply pined to return to Spain, so I came back, bought a state-of-the-art vehicle and began to ply my trade, stopping wherever I wished and… reconnecting with my past."

"What past?"

"My time here, of course. The most formative years of my far from dull life. So what do you really think of my selling fireworks, Marta?" I asked, as I knew that Harry would subject me to a far more arduous interrogation and Laura would… well, I had no idea how she would react, but revealing my make-believe career would be a calculated risk, though a selfless one, as if she really was a key player in Hugo's dodgy dealings I felt that Harry had a right to know. When I denied having worked for Hugo and told them about rockets, bangers and sparklers instead, I would watch her reaction closely and if I detected so much as a hint of perplexity I'd have to tell Harry that he may be throwing in his lot with a wily outlaw rather than the retired diplomat that he thought he'd landed. She might be on the phone to Hugo like a shot and jeopardise my involvement in the forthcoming truffle bonanza, but friendship comes before riches in my book, and besides, maybe I really could make a go of my fireworks enterprise and thus extricate myself from a commitment that might land me in the soup, but back to my guinea pig, Marta.

"I don't know, Chef. Is there any future in fireworks? Is it even safe to carry a lot of them in a van?"

"Perfectly safe, if one knows how to handle them."

"Hmm, but one reads in the newspapers about explosions in firework factories."

"Carelessness or insurance scams. Tell me, Marta, what kind of fireworks do people here usually buy?"

"None."

"None?"

"None. The city council brings in experts for the fiestas and other functions. I suppose the kids buy firecrackers to play the fool with, but most people don't buy fireworks. This is why I'm surprised at your choice of activity, Chef."

I was going to ask her about Guy Fawkes Night, before remembering that it was a purely British affair and that Guy and his papist pals were probably financed by a Spain still smarting from our annihilation of their armada, but this was no time for a history lesson, so I asked Marta how things had gone for her over the years.

"Oh, I met my husband, Juan Ramón, a while after you left and we eventually married. We took over the bar when my father died – my mother is well and comes in occasionally – and have had two children, María and Francisco, who are both at university now."

"Please give my regards to your mother."

"I will. I expect you are wondering what has become of Carmela, Chef."

I *had* been wondering about my former sweetheart, but mainly, since meeting Marta, about her size. Had she also ballooned to alarming proportions? If so, it would put my mind at rest that I'd made the correct decision to flee, but how was I to procure this sensitive information without offending my hefty hostess?

"Yes. I assume she has also married and had children."

"That's right. After you left she was depressed for a while."

I nodded gravely. "Understandable, I suppose."

"Yes, because it was awkward for her to have been friendly with someone who… well, was forced to leave by the backdoor. Although she insisted that the two of you had been little more than friends, for a long time no local men wished to have anything to do with her and it was beginning to look like she would end up on the shelf."

"Right."

"Anyway, it was after she had finally got her teeth fixed that a man walked into the fishmonger's where she worked. Well, love blossomed and they were married just six months later."

"I see. Does she still work at the fishmonger's?"

"Oh no, her husband was a builder and he didn't want her to continue working."

"Ah, so I suppose she became a housewife while he continued to work on site. I hope he isn't one of those builders who go to the bar after work and arrive home drunk for dinner and throw their filthy clothes on the floor," I said, rueing her sad fate and what might have been had she not driven me away.

"Ha, no, no, he wasn't the kind of builder who got his hands dirty."

"Did he wear gloves?"

"Yes, he favoured deerskin gloves at the time, but they left Jaén soon after they were married. They lived in Madrid for many years, but by the time of the crisis of 2008 he had made so much money that he was able to retire. They live on Lanzarote now, in a huge chalet with a pool, though they also have a farmhouse in Asturias and an apartment in Paris."

"Paris?"

"Yes, their daughter, Eugenia, wished to study there, so they bought a little place near the Sorbonne. Their son, Borja, is also very clever and has just become a notary, so everything has worked out well for Carmela in the end, thank goodness. She visits her family here at Christmastime and I must say that despite her wealth she's still very down to earth. Would you like to see a photograph taken here last winter?"

"Yes," I said, as by now I was almost willing Carmela to have become as fat as Marta, I'm slightly ashamed to admit.

She lumbered over to the bar and returned with a large photograph. "Here we are, the two of us, just six months ago."

I focussed on the slim, elegant woman with her arm around Marta's blubbery neck. Like me, she appeared to have scarcely aged at all, though unlike me she wore makeup and I suspected that her hair had been dyed. Still, she cut quite a figure beside Marta, who one might have assumed to be a favourite servant.

"Very nice," I said, handing back the photo.

"Have you noticed her arm?" she said, pointing to the one around her neck.

"Ah, yes."

"You'll remember that it used to be slightly withered, though she could hold the fish well enough while she chopped them. Well, that turned out to be a problem of trapped nerves which a surgeon in America was able to rectify. Now it's almost as strong as her right arm and doesn't dangle by her side like it used to."

"I'm delighted for her," I said, amazed that Marta had made so much of a trifling defect that had been hardly noticeable. Maybe she was jealous of her success, I conjectured, while my feeling was one of pure relief that she had overcome her disappointment and had had the tremendous good fortune to meet a successful speculator, regardless of how he had come by his money, for I wasn't one to moralise in this respect, having just made a packet, I hoped, by means that would make a mere builder quake in his boots.

"I'd better be off now, Marta, as I have people to see," I said, taking out my wallet.

She flapped her hand. "Don't be silly, Chef, this is on me. Ah, just like in the old days when we fed you at the end of the month, eh?"

"Yes, your parents were kind to me," I said, recalling the odd outstanding tab, nothing more. Marta's memory was both hazy and inventive, and after planting two kisses on her flabby cheeks I left the place feeling worried that senile dementia might be just around the corner for that kindly but deluded woman.

Discarding my disguise, I spent the rest of the day wandering from bar to bar to escape the heat, so by the time I reached Peñamefécit at 1915 hours I felt rather tipsy and was sorely tempted to climb into the back of Bambi and enjoy a belated siesta. This, however, would have been imprudent, so I retrieved the key, started her up and drove my newly nippy van up to the modern university, where I parked up, hopped in the back – rueing Bambi's slightly crushed posterior – and stuck my hand under the cushions. I calmly opened the brown envelope and was pleased to find notes to the value of six thousand euros (€6000), a fair payment for my perilous journey which would enable me to buy me plenty of fireworks, if I did eventually decide to go down the pyrotechnic route, as Marta's reaction to my fictitious career had been far from positive. Content with my day's work, I lay down on the bed for a short snooze before heading for the open road once more.

7

In the event I slept soundly until eight o'clock the next morning, so after visiting a nearby bar for breakfast and to make use their restroom, I headed back towards Granada, planning to spend the night in the wonderful city that I'd always planned to visit. On reaching the outskirts of that monumental marvel, however, my mobile phone rang for the first time on Spanish soil and I saw that it was Harry himself who was calling, but as I was driving on a dual-carriageway and reluctant to break the law I let it ring. This was a wise decision, I soon realised, as before speaking to that uncultured though cunning man I ought to get the story of my first weeks in Spain straight in my head. As the Granada exit lay up ahead I turned off and headed into the city, where I parked Bambi on the outskirts, to save on parking, and strolled into the centre.

On spotting an *Oficina de Turismo* I wandered in and it was there among those stacks of leaflets that I had my first brainwave of the day. I could tell Harry that after meeting Hugo briefly we had decided to postpone my debut until after the summer, so after relaxing on the coast for a while I had come to Granada to... do what? Realising that my brainwave was still in its embryonic stage

I concluded that I had to do two things before speaking to my fat friend; get to know the city well, and settle on a believable occupation, as by then I'd slept on fireworks and dismissed them as a product likely to provoke a sceptical reaction, as even the muddled Marta had disparaged the idea. So, after grabbing one of every single leaflet in the place, much to the annoyance of the po-faced assistant, I popped them into my handy knapsack and set off to gain inspiration in the shopping streets. After dawdling in front of an E-Cigarette shop for a while I dismissed their products as being noxious and insufficiently showy, but when I entered the Alcaicería, a street full of souvenir shops on the site of the old Arab bazaar, my mind was immediately stimulated by the array of products on offer. I feasted my eyes on Arabic craftwork, lamps, trinkets, pictures, jewellery and weird clothing, as well as many tacky modern items, but it was the rugs that grabbed my attention; rugs of all shapes and sizes – though mainly rectangular – with myriad designs woven from wool, cotton, silk and goodness knows what else.

As I wandered from shop to shop I gradually realised that rugs were just the thing for me to deal in. They were bulky, colourful, attractive, pleasant to handle and could be rolled out with a flourish for prospective customers and potential cynics like Harry, as even he couldn't fail to be impressed by such an aesthetically pleasing sight spilling out of the back of Bambi. Rugs had *presence* and before the day was out I resolved to acquire half a vanful of them, as the other half would suffice for my living quarters. Had I disposed of more time I suppose I could have located a wholesaler, but the longer I delayed calling Harry back, the more he would suspect that I wasn't prospering, so I returned to the first shop on the row and set about haggling with a vengeance.

I'm certain that in the old days, especially before 1492 when the Christians muscled back into the city, haggling was the order of the day and that many a bargain was to be had by the persistent punter, but alas in the internet age we seem to have lost our inclination to engage in that charming practice. When I offered the shopkeepers or their assistants half the stated price, just to get the ball rolling, they merely eyed me with disdain and hurried away to sell a calendar to a Japanese or a bracelet to a Swede, and I reached the other end of the row without a rug to my name. While fingering my bulky wallet – though I'd hidden most of my money in my shoes, giving me a pleasantly elevated feeling – I realised that I was going about things the wrong way, so I retraced my steps and started again using the following astute method.

"Buenos días, I wish to purchase a selection of rugs," I said to the first shopkeeper, a squat, swarthy man who may have been of Berber origin.

"Yes, you called in not long ago," he replied with ruffled brow and suspicious eyes.

I then counted out twenty €100 notes onto the counter. "I need a collection of colourful rugs right away. What can you give me for two thousand euros?"

The sight of the cash certainly grabbed his attention, but just as he began to stroke the first rug that came to hand I folded the notes in half and slowly slipped them back into my wallet, leaving half an inch or so sticking out at the top. I smiled serenely and waggled the wallet to and fro before his goggling eyes.

"I no longer have time to haggle, my man. I'm going to visit every shop on the street which has a worthwhile stock of rugs and make the same offer to each proprietor. I will then revisit each establishment and see who can offer me the brightest, bulkiest and best quality assortment for my money. Hasta pronto, amigo," I said, before saluting with my wallet and turning to leave.

"But wait, señor," said the now suitably servile little chappie.

I paused, turned, raised my eyebrows and pursed my lips.

"Bright is no problem, but which is most important for you, quality or bulk?"

"Quality."

"Right."

"Yes, bulky quality. I want to see a great big pile of top-notch rugs when I come back."

"What do you want them for?"

"None of your business. Now get going," I said, before striding out of the shop and into the next one.

Of the five shops that I chose, for I didn't want to put anyone out unnecessarily, two more owners were as keen as the first, while the fourth insisted that I stay to select the rugs and the final one gazed at me mutely for so long that I turned on my heels and stomped out. Of the three remaining candidates for my hard-earned dosh the first proved to have outshone the others, presenting me with a handsome pile of about thirty rugs, none of them overlarge, but of all the colours of the rainbow and then some, so I snapped a photo of them with my phone and told him I'd be returning presently in my vehicle for him to load them in. About an hour later, having finally come to terms with the torturous one-way system, the deal was completed and he and his assistant loaded the right-hand side of Bambi with the merchandise that would make Harry's beady eyes pop open in admiration.

"The little van will lean, señor," said the fortunate vendor. "Better to use all the space, I think."

"And where am I going to sleep, prey?"

He just shrugged, shook my proffered hand and walked away with a spring in his step, the lucky devil.

So, armed with my hypothetical livelihood, all that remained was to gen up on the city, which I did in half an hour after driving a listing Bambi back to the suburbs. My swotting done, I repaired to a park bench to ring Harry.

"Harry? Hi, sorry I couldn't take your call earlier. I was in a meeting. Are you and Laura at the house?" I said in a loud – for he is partially deaf – but not over-exuberant way, as Harry, for all his limitations, had spent his whole working life sniffing out bullshit and had become rather good at it.

"Yep, arrived yesterday."

"Good, good, I'll come up and see you as soon as I can. I'm in Granada on business just now."

"Right," he said, and nothing more, so, realising that he hoped to draw me out by means of succinct replies, I decided to play him at his own game.

"Yep, nice here."

"Grand."

"I'll be done soon. Shall I come up the day after tomorrow?"

"Yep, that'll be fine."

"Did Laura like the Lakes?"

"Loved 'em."

"Great."

"Do you remember the way?"

"Of course. You know me."

"That's why I asked. Bambi still going?"

"Like a dream."

"See you Saturday then. We'll be in from dinner time onwards."

"Meaning lunchtime?"

"Yep."

"Until then."

"Bye."

After hanging up I returned to the van and gathered together the recently perused leaflets that were strewn all over the rugs, before deciding to leave the city and make tracks towards the coast. In the end I had to follow the shopkeeper's advice and redistribute my rugs, as Bambi lurched dangerously on every right-hand bend, but once I'd set her on an even keel I made good time and reached Almuñécar before nightfall. I checked into a campsite just off the main road and, after parking on my pitch, immediately broke out in a cold sweat, or a tepid one, as although Claudia would have expected me to return to the same campsite in Torre del Mar for debriefing, it wasn't the end of the world as I could check in the following day and leave a message for her if she didn't turn up, having no intention of hanging around there until she deigned to drop by.

While drying my forehead with my right hand I fondled the rugs with my left, and it occurred to me that perhaps the time was ripe for me to sever my ties with her and Hugo and go it alone. Despite splashing out on my stock I was still mucked up with money, so much so that I even thought about opening a bank account, but to do that I'd have to have an address, as although Bambi was a home she most certainly wasn't a house. Laura's house would be a handy postal address, but first I'd have to ensure that she wasn't trapped in Hugo's labyrinthine web of lawlessness, so I spent some time musing over how best to draw her out, before concluding that I'd have to play it by ear and hope for the best. As for me, well, would I be capable of making a go of my incipient enterprise and sell enough rugs to keep body and soul together? Undoubtedly, I concluded, but could even large-scale rug sales ever match the fortune I stood to make by transporting truffles? Decidedly not, I thought, and as truffles – unlike illicit tobacco, illegal immigrants and weapons – were only food, what was the worst that could happen if I were caught? A slap on the wrist? A tax bill? Ha, child's play to a desperado like me.

No, or rather yes, I'd be well-advised to stick with the slippery Belgian until the truffle season was over and I'd made enough money to buy that chalet I mentioned, with an infinity pool and a carport under which Bambi and maybe a mid-range Porsche could shelter from the sun's rays. Happy with the outcome of my *sotto voce* question and answer session, which I've elucidated so you may see how my dialectical mind works, I heated up the last two tins of Harry's emergency store (chicken curry and ravioli), washed them down with a bottle of white wine, lugged the rugs off my bed, and settled down for a well-earned night's kip.

The following morning, sunny once more, I set off early and reached the Laguna Beach campsite before ten, where the pretty but straitlaced receptionist welcomed me back with open arms, figuratively speaking, before informing me that I had no messages and telling me that if I wished to check in before midday I'd have to pay for another night.

"Why so, light of my life?" I asked chirpily.

"Because the new day begins at noon."

"Come, come, surely a couple of hours don't matter, seeing as I'll be staying for a fortnight this time."

"All right then, but please don't pester the women again."

"Pester or bedazzle?" I quipped, for I was in a heartily good mood.

"Just behave. Do you want to pay now?"

"In a while, dear. I'll just check that there's a pitch to my liking," I said, and I shimmied out feeling pretty pleased with myself about not paying for an extra night, despite the fact that I'd be off the following morning, until I remembered that I might well have to leave a message for Claudia in trustworthy hands. Rather than going back and coughing up for the two nights, or waiting outside until twelve like a sad scrooge, I decided to settle in and just hope that Claudia would put in an appearance. By two my golden-brown skin had taken about as much sun as it could handle, so after a plunge in the pool I decided to don my panama hat, plus clothes of course, and wander into town for a bite to eat, as Claudia was unlikely to appear in the afternoon.

After a light lunch the sky clouded over, so I began to stroll along the seafront and before I knew it I found myself heading in the direction of Hugo's house. Nonplussed by my autonomous limbs, I allowed them to lope on along the lane until it dawned on me why they were conveying me towards my employer's house; because I hadn't clapped eyes on him since my return to Spain and it was about time I gave him a chance to thank me for my valiant missions. Whether he'd be pleased to see me or not was another matter, but a quick glance at the carport would tell me if the balding Belgian was in residence, and at that point I could decide whether to announce myself or discretely toddle back to the campsite. Nothing ventured, nothing gained, a favourite teacher of mine used to say, though he later drowned attempting to swim across the English Channel.

As I neared the gates I saw they were securely padlocked, but the red Twingo was parked in the exact same spot, looking dustier than ever. Beside it there was a white, dust-free Volvo, and on the other side a similarly clean black Mazda MX-5, so I surmised that the Belgian was back but had tightened his belt until the good times returned, maybe right away given that his faithful lieutenant, namely me, had pulled off the gun run without a hitch. After vacillating for a while the prudent part of my brain told me to clear off, as I'd had clear instructions never to call round, while the proud and fearless part willed me to ring the intercom, for I am nobody's lackey and come and go as I jolly well please. In the end I compromised by pressing the button very quickly, allowing fate to decree whether they'd hear my rapid ring or not.

As no sound of movement reached me through the still, sultry air I was about to depart when I heard the click of a latch and on seeing a shadowy figure appear in the doorway I waved my hat and peered through the bars. On perceiving that it was none other than the delicious Claudia, I yoo-hooed her heartily, upon which she threw her hands to her head, patted her hair with her fists and came running towards me.

"I was just passing and decided to drop–" I began.

"Shush, you imbecile," she interjected, before scaling the gate like a squirrel, landing softly by my side and leading me off down the lane at a great rate of knots.

"As I say, I was just–"

"What in God's name are you doing here, you damned moron?" she said, or words to that effect, before steering me onto a field and shoving me between two orange trees, which though fragrant wouldn't be ripe for the picking for some time.

"Can a man not go for an afternoon stroll, my dear?" I said with a soothing smile intended to ameliorate her mood.

"Not down this lane, you can't. Now what the hell do you want, you blasted buffoon?"

I patted her arm. "Sticks and stones, Claudia, sticks and stones."

"What *are* you on about?"

"Nothing. Er, it occurred to me that Hugo might want to… debrief me."

"Debrief you? He'll bloody behead you if he sees you here. *None* of his operatives come here, unless it's absolutely essential."

"Then what brings you here, pray?"

Her face clouded and she examined my sandals. "I… I just called round to… drop something off."

I grinned knowingly. "The gun money, eh?"

"That's right. Well done, by the way."

By way of reply I looked away and shrugged modestly.

"Look, you must go in a moment. I was going to come to the campsite tomorrow morning, but I might as well tell you now. Hugo won't be needing you again until Project T begins."

I nodded and emitted a mirthless snort.

"I'll contact you shortly before your first assignment."

"How? I don't intend to fester in that infernal campsite for the whole summer, you know. I plan to take to the road and... er, travel," I said, managing to avoid mentioning the rugs in the nick of time, as it was no business of hers.

"Well, I'll... call you then. Do you have a mobile?"

"Yes, an English one."

"Oh... great. The police can't trace those, so it'll be safe," she said, whipping a pen from her shorts pocket.

I dictated the number, including the prefix, and as I did so my blood began to boil, or at least simmer, for it seemed to me that she was casting me off like an old dishcloth. Just when we had some downtime in which to get to know each other better and maybe explore the sierras in Bambi for a few days, she was fobbing me off as if I were some seedy old no-hoper. No, this simply wouldn't do, so after expanding my chest and stretching to my full height I stamped symbolically on the ground.

"Have you got cramp?"

"No, I haven't got cramp," I hissed, pushing a branchful of unripe oranges away, only for them to bounce back and clatter me on the head. "I want to see Hugo. I've pulled off two daring missions while he'd been sitting on his arse and it's about time he showed his appreciation."

"Hasn't he done that already?" she asked, rubbing her finger and thumb together.

"It's... it's not just about the money, Claudia. I've always taken pride in my work and I *demand* to see the man who's raking it in thanks to me," I said, with one foot slightly in front of the other and my hands on my hips, as forthright body language is essential when laying down the law. "Lead me to him," I growled, before stomping off, tripping over an exposed root, and miraculously staying on two feet.

Claudia smiled, but I could see that it was a smile applied in order to conceal some deep-seated misgivings. I had her on the back foot and meant to press my advantage home, so when she tried to take my arm I deftly freed myself and sprinted back to the lane like a man half my age. As Claudia *was* half my age, or slightly less, she managed to head me off and as she stood panting in the lane my anger turned into desire, as she looked like a Latin Queen Boadicea, though without the crown, or the chariot.

"Stand aside, you strumpet!" I cried, feeling that a spot of stern ribaldry was in order.

"Geoff, please," she pleaded.

"I *shall* see that blighter Hugo!" I roared, proceeding to brush her aside.

The fact that she then encircled me with her strong but slender arms and pulled me despairingly to her made me relent, and a moment later we were embracing like feverish lovers.

"Oh, Claudia!" I gasped.

"Oh, Geoff!" she panted, holding me away from her and gazing so longingly into my eyes that I knew she'd been engulfed by the same smouldering passion that had set my blood coursing through my veins, mostly in one direction.

"Claudia, come to Bambi! I mean to ravish you."

"Oh, not now, Geoff!" she gasped.

"Then when, my love?"

"Soon, soon. I'll call you, I promise, but you must go now. Hugo is… is in a crucial meeting and to disturb him now could be critical for all of us. Any other time he'd have been delighted to see you – he said so only yesterday – but right now our futures lie in the balance. Please go now."

"I shall, but tell me, with whom is our brave boss in conference?"

"I can't tell you that," she mumbled, still in my grasp.

"It's not that fiend Axel, is it?"

"What? Oh… yes, yes, it's him, Axel. He's come to… talk things over."

"Is Hugo in danger? Can I help? Let us fly!" I declaimed, getting quite carried away by this dramatic turn of events.

"No, no danger, unless Axel smells a rat," she said as I slipped my arm around her waist, subconsciously suspecting that I'd be as well to make the most of this unexpected clinch.

"Go now, dear, and I'll call you soon," she begged.

"All right," I said, stroking her hair. "All good things come to him who waits. Tomorrow I drive to Canillas to visit Harry and Laura, but my mobile will never leave my side."

She seemed to shiver, before grasping my arm. "Laura?"

"And Harry, my English pal, remember?"

"Yes, yes," she said, before becoming rather pensive, so I moved my hands to her shoulders and kneaded them softly while I waited.

"A penny for your thoughts?" I said.

"What?"

"What are you thinking, sweetie?"

"Oh, nothing. Hugo confirmed that Laura's just a friend, by the way, but please don't blab about your activities."

I tapped my nose and tipped my hat back with the same agile finger. "Ha, that's the last thing I'd do," I said, suddenly seeing Harry's ghostly face over her shoulder, in my mind's eye.

"Good. What will you tell them you've been up to?"

Harry's face turned into a rug, so I decided there'd be no harm in telling her about my little sideline. Besides, I didn't want her to think that her future lover lacked initiative and was content to wait around until the truffle business commenced.

"Well," I began, stroking her neck with one hand and her arm with the other; storing up tactile memories, so to speak. "I've just purchased a load of rugs in Granada at a knockdown price. I intend to sell them in the villages that I visit on my forthcoming motor tour; a tour, I might add, that you're welcome to come on."

"I'd love to, Geoff, I really would," she said, peeling my hand from her neck and clasping it. "I'll try to join you for a few days in August, but I can't promise anything yet. So, do you have a lot of rugs in the van?"

"Yes, a kaleidoscopic stock of quality rugs from every corner of the globe. They cost me two thousand, but I'll quadruple my money, I'm sure."

"Hmm, listen, why don't you tell Laura and your friend that you've been selling rugs for a while?"

"Oh, Claudia, great minds and twin souls think alike!" I gushed, moving my free hand to her waist and guiding her through a few waltz steps.

"Do they?" she replied, smiling as she let herself be led, so I slid us seamlessly into a tango.

"Yes, that's my exact intention, to tell them I've been peddling rugs ever since I arrived. Harry's a nosy devil, you see, so I mean to cover my trail with a constant stream of rug talk," I said, switching subtly to the lambada, at which point she prised herself free and brought us to a halt.

"That's brilliant, Geoff. Listen, if Laura does mention Hugo, just tell her that you met him once when you got here and that you both agreed to wait a while before beginning to work together."

"Snap!"

"What?"

"That's precisely what I plan to say. Quick meeting, nothing on for the summer, so I thought on my feet and got into the rug trade."

"Wonderful, and please stick to that story. Hugo's incommunicado right now, as you know, so if she tries she won't be able to get hold of him."

"I'll explain."

"Explain what?"

"That he's incommunicado."

"But you can't, you… silly thing. You don't *know* what he's doing, because you saw him just once, several weeks ago. Please get that straight in your head. One visit, then rugs. Is that clear?"

"Perfectly."

"And I don't even exist, of course. If they ask you about women, invent a story about one you met at the campsite or something."

I chuckled gutturally. "Ha, what makes you think I'll have to *invent* a story? I've been a free agent until today, remember, but the others are as nothing compared to you and from now on I will remain as faithful as a… horse."

She gave me a lovingly quizzical look. "Er, right. Now, off you go. I'll call you as soon as I can."

I ran the tip of my tongue languorously along my top lip. "I can soon unload those rugs to make room for you, you know."

"I swear I'll try to join you at some stage, now please be off."

I ran my tongue back the other way, before wiggling it about. "How about a little au revoir kiss, my precious?"

She then screwed up her eyes with desire and planted a moist but tongueless kiss on my lips, before breaking free, running back to the gate and clambering over it like a woman possessed, fearing, perchance, for her chastity, because that clumsy kiss had told me that her sexual experience was minimal, which I didn't mind, quite the contrary, as I've run in more than one neophyte in my time.

"Farewell, my love!" I hollered.

"Adiós, Geoff, and stick to your story."

"Like a limpet."

"What?"

"I will," I assured her, before blowing her one last kiss and striding away, my head held high.

On the long walk back I felt hot in every sense of the word, but after a delicious dip in the pool I became serene enough to lay down for a siesta on a Moroccan rug I rolled out in the shade beside Bambi. When the sun had cooled a little I entered my sanctuary and tossed and turned for a while longer, fitfully dreaming of sundry scenes in which Claudia and I both featured – on the beach, in the pool, up a mountain, at the dinner table, in bed together – but in each and every situation Harry's shiny head and leering face popped up at some point, so when I awoke in a hot sweat I swore on Claudia's life to stick to my rug story like superglue, lest he winkle out the truth and cause me no end of bother.

8

The following morning I drove to reception, nipped inside, slapped a fifty euro note down on the desk, winked at the frosty little wench and roared out of the gates never to return. Noisy, humid, seaside campsites are all very well for a while, but I was pining for the hills, so after filling Bambi's radiator and fuel tank I steered her up the long and winding road to Canillas, where I found Laura's white house at the top of the village on the third trip around its sinuous streets. I parked against the same wall as on our previous visit and spent some time breathing in the warm, clean mountain air before strolling over to the door.

'I met Hugo once, I don't know Claudia, I sell rugs," I said to myself as I rang the bell, and a moment later the chubby figure of Laura stood before me, looking tanned, healthy and ever so pleased to see me.

"Hello, Geoff, do come in," she said, in English, which I didn't mind as she was Belgian and there wasn't a hope in hell that Harry would ever learn Spanish.

After bestowing two kisses on my silky-smooth cheeks she led me through the house to the small pool, where I found Harry basking like a pink porpoise, glass of beer in hand.

"Ah, there you are," he said, without getting up.

"Yes," I replied, aware that his noncommittal statement was his artless way of drawing me out, so I turned to Laura, who wore smart shorts and a sleeveless top and had already sat down in the shade of a parasol. I couldn't help comparing her tanned but slightly flabby arms to those of Claudia, the thought of whom made me forget the commonplace comment I'd been about to utter, so eager was I to temporarily erase her memory from my rug seller's mind.

"Cat got your tongue?" said Harry, swinging his elephantine legs off the sunbed and prising his sweaty back from the canvas.

"No, no, merely tired after a sleepless night," I improvised, before yawning to underline the point.

"Been living it up down there at the beach, have you?"

"Yes. That's to say, yes and no. Last night I had a tryst with a young lady in Torre del Mar, but I've been all over the place, selling my merchandise."

"Cars?" he asked.

"No, Hugo and I haven't started working together just yet, so I've set up a little concern of my own."

"Ha, I knew it. So his promise to pay you a grand a month was bullshit after all. Didn't I tell you, Laura?"

"Yes, but Hugo never mentioned that to me. To tell you the truth, Geoff, I'm a little concerned about Hugo. The last few times I've tried to call him he didn't reply."

"I expect he's busy," I said, before breathing deeply in and out through my nostrils in order to refresh the supply of blood to my brain, just in case.

"He usually is, but whenever I leave a message on his answerphone he always calls back eventually."

I cleared my throat and avoided Harry's inquisitive eyes. "Well, I just saw him once, the day after I arrived. He said things were quiet and promised to call me when they picked up. That's why I got into rugs," I said, hoping to divert their attention away from Hugo.

"Rugs?" Laura asked, right on cue.

"Yes, I began to–"

"Wait a minute," said Harry, raising his hand. "Hugo promised you work. That's what you told Jeremy and me. Then he went back on his word. He's also stopped answering the phone to Laura. Now, either of those things could be easily explained, especially the one about employing you, but for *both* of these things to have happened at the same time is odd, very odd indeed. I smell a rat."

"Oh, I'll call him again soon," said Laura. "I'm sure there'll be some explanation."

"Geoff, have you called him recently?"

"No, I don't... there's been no need."

"I don't what?" he growled, standing up and approaching my chair, effectively eclipsing the sun.

"I don't... have his number," I said, his pop-eyed stare robbing me of my imaginative powers, but I rallied. "He's got my number, so I don't need his, you see."

"Very odd." He turned to Laura. "Don't you think that's odd, love?"

"Hmm, a little, but Hugo can be a little secretive at times. I once arrived for lunch when there were several cars there. He hurried out, jumped in beside me and took me to a restaurant in town. I've told you before that his business may be a little... what was that word you used?"

"Dodgy?" Harry said.

"That's right, dodgy. You know, I sometimes think that Geoff might be better off doing his own thing."

"That's what I thought," I said, having staved off a cold sweat by the skin of my... skin.

"Tell us about these rugs of yours, Geoff," she said, so I adeptly transposed my Granada purchase to an earlier date.

"You *what*?" said my potential nemesis. "You bought a load of rugs from a *shop*?"

"Yes," I said with a grin, happy for him to needle me about rugs till the cows came home, as long as he stayed off the subject of Hugo, for he was quite capable of insisting on driving down there to hunt him out, so strong are his policing instincts, despite never having risen above the rank of bog-standard bobby.

"How the heck are you going to make a profit then, you numpty?"

"Ah, but I bought in bulk and haggled till the poor chap was blue in the face."

"How many did you buy?"

"About thir... fifty."

"Thir-fifty? What's that when it's at home?"

"Thirty the first time, twenty the second," I said, quick as a flash. "I've sold about twenty, so I've still got about thirty left."

"Ab*ou*t? Do you not keep stock of what you've got?"

I swatted the air and smiled. "Oh, it's just a sideline. I drive about from place to place, sell a rug here and there, you know, just getting by and reconnecting with Spain."

"Hmm," he hemmed sceptically, before brightening up. "Ha, to really reconnect you'll have to go to Jaén one day, eh? To see your old flame."

On feeling the blood rise to my face, I took a sip of the beer that Laura had just brought me and remarked on the heat.

"Have a swim, Geoff, then we'll have lunch," said my charmingly uninquisitive hostess.

While we ate the cottage pie that Harry had taught Laura how to make, I asked them all about their stay in Lancaster and especially about their trip to the Lake District. Not wishing to stray from the subject, I quizzed them about every single day of their holiday, and while Laura answered happily, Harry's replies were brief and I could tell that his small but active brain was still engaged on other matters. As Laura told me about Windermere, Coniston, Keswick and so on it occurred to me that I'd better give some thought to my supposed rug-selling route, so after lunch I excused myself and went to my well-appointed bedroom for a siesta, where instead of sleeping I perused my map of Andalucía and made many a mental note, plus a few written ones in case I forgot where I'd supposedly been touting my wares.

When I emerged some time later I found Harry and Laura canoodling in the pool, so I discreetly backtracked into the house, as the sight of all that mature flesh splashing around seemed somehow indecent, though I don't suppose Laura's all that much older than me, in years. When they'd heaved themselves out of the water I sallied forth and we soon settled down to coffee and biscuits, as Harry can't go for more than three hours without shovelling something into his gob. As we sipped and munched away I was keen to elaborate on the subject of my rug sales while my itinerary was still fresh in my mind, but Harry would insist on going over the whole Hugo business again, as when a man has no hobbies his working life tends to spill over into his retirement years, for want of anything better to think about.

"I reckon that if he doesn't answer you in the next few days we ought to drive down there and find out what's what," said the sleuth in conclusion to his tedious hypothesising.

"All right, Harry," said Laura, who, it must be said, has the patience of a saint. "Now, Geoff, tell us all about this rug business. I'm dying to know how you've been getting on."

I cleared the old throat. "Well," I began, and proceeded to talk them through my leisurely route around the villages of Malaga, including Riogordo and Colmenar, which I'd driven through, and

Villanueva de la Concepción, La Joya, Los Nogales, Valle de Abdalajís, El Chorro, Carratraca, Álora and Pizarra, which I certainly hadn't, but I'd spent two hours memorising their names so I was damned if I was going to miss any out. I told them that after camping in the country I'd usually driven Bambi into a village square in the cool of the morning and had chatted nonchalantly to the locals in the bar, before subtly bringing up the subject of rugs, after which I'd lured a few of them out to peruse my wares, before selling an average of two rugs in each place, in order to achieve the grand total of twenty that Harry was unlikely to have forgotten.

"The rest of the time I went walking, ate wholesome meals and generally just chilled out up there in the sierra. Then I drove back to Granada to replenish my stock, which is when you called me," I said, tremendously pleased with my astonishing feat of memory.

"It sounds great," said Laura. "I have a good friend called Justine who lives in Valle de Abdalajís. She moved there from Brussels shortly after I came here."

Damn Justine, I thought, as although that dratted village had been by far the hardest to memorise, I knew sod all about the place.

"Ah," I said.

"What's it like, love?" Harry asked her, his eyes glued to mine.

"Oh, it's a large village beside an imposing peak that I believe people like to climb."

"Did you climb it, Geoff?"

"No, not that one. It looked a bit tricky to me," I said, my fingers crossed tightly under the table.

"Oh, yes, it's ever so steep and high. I think you need ropes and things to climb it from the village," said my unwitting saviour, and I swore there and then that I *would* visit the place, if only to pay homage to the hill that got Harry off my back, as had he sniffed the merest whiff of uncertainty he'd have quizzed me about every single place I hadn't visited until he'd torn my mythical route to shreds, after which he'd have dug deeper still until through sheer exhaustion I'd have spilled the beans about all my capers. It was a great relief when he went inside to shave and shower, and though I was dying for a dip I braced myself for the final onerous task of my stay, touch wood, which was to reassure myself of Laura's innocence regarding Hugo's crooked career.

I poured us each a little more coffee, before settling back in my chair, putting my hands behind my head, looking at the lovely view, and sighing.

"It's nice here, isn't it, Laura?"

"Yes, I love it, and now that Harry's here it's even better. We'll go for a walk early tomorrow morning, if you like. We could do a different route to the one we did last time you were here."

"I'd like that," I said. "Being up here one feels far away from the sordid world down there, doesn't one?"

"Er, yes, I suppose one does."

"I mean, just think of all the crime that's occurring as we sit here sipping coffee. Only the other day, in Carratraca, I saw the police arrest a man with a van full of smuggled tobacco," I said, eying her closely through my sunglasses. "It's terrible what people will do to make a living."

"Yes, though it was an odd place to catch him."

"Why's that?"

"Well, it's right off the beaten track, isn't it? And I don't think Carratraca is a very big place, though I've never been."

"Where would you take smuggled cigarettes, Laura?" I asked. "Just for the sake of argument," I added, on seeing her perturbed expression.

"Well, I imagine they get them from Gibraltar, or so I've heard, and as cigarettes aren't too dear in Spain I guess they take them to northern Europe, maybe to your country."

"Hmm, I suppose so. More coffee?"

"No thanks, Geoff. Don't drink too much more, as it's quite strong."

"Something else that really concerns me are all these poor immigrants coming over the straits to Spain in all sorts of boats."

"Oh, yes, it's awful!" she said with what appeared to be genuine concern. "Do you know what I think we should do?"

"Er, help them through Spain in little vans?"

"What? No, no, that just exacerbates the problem. As a former diplomat I'm quite well-informed about international affairs and greater minds than mine have argued that what the First World has to do is improve conditions in Third World countries. You know, make serious investments in infrastructure and enable more companies to establish themselves there. It depends, of course, on if the governments of those countries will cooperate or merely try to enrich themselves, but surely it's worth a try. Oh, if there weren't so much greed in the world everybody could enjoy a reasonable standard of living. Globalisation could have such a positive effect, if only the Western World used its power in the right way, don't you agree?"

I stifled a yawn. "Yes," I said, fearing that she might be trying to distract me. "Another big problem is arms smuggling."

"I'm sorry?"

"You know, smuggling weapons."

"Oh, right, but what's that got to do with what we're talking about, Geoff?" she said, her brow furrowing like a concertina.

"Oh, because you mentioned globalisation, I guess. Did you know that heinous organisations are smuggling arms through

Spain in vans as we speak?" I said, deftly flipping up my sunglasses and gazing into her brown Belgian eyes.

"Er... no, I didn't know that," she said, staring at my coffee cup into which I'd poured only a drop of brandy. "I wonder what's taking Harry so long."

Feeling that I'd grilled her sufficiently and by now convinced that she knew nothing of Hugo's evil empire, I became worried that my subtle interrogation might get back to Harry; something I hadn't thought of when I began to put her on the spot. If she told him I'd been harping on about felonious forms of making money he'd immediately smell one of his rats and give me the third degree until I cracked, so I had to somehow explain why I'd brought up the subject of crime, and fast, as though Harry is a sluggish man, even he ought to have performed his ablutions by now.

I cleared my throat. "I mentioned crime because it's surprising the stories one hears when one is on the road," I said.

"Really?"

"Yes, I got into many conversations in the village bars and this subject came up time and time again."

"Oh, I thought men normally talked about football," she said with a nervous chuckle.

"Yes... Yes! Yes, they do, but as I'm not interested in football the talk soon turns to crime. One chap in Colmenar told me all about cigarette smuggling. It appears to be rife there."

"I see, though I'd never have guessed. Did you visit Carratraca after Colmenar?"

I pursed my lips and reviewed my route. "Yes, a few days later. Why do you ask?"

"Well, it was in Carratraca where you saw the police arresting a man with tobacco. That must have felt like quite a coincidence."

I twitched my sunglasses back over my eyes. I'd forgotten about the arrest and couldn't recall where it had happened. If she'd been Harry she'd have tried to trick me by naming a different village, but had she been with him for long enough to have picked up his devious ways?

"Yes," I said, nodding slowly. "Yes, it was."

"Maybe you should move your chair into the shade, Geoff. The evening sun can be deceptively hot."

I did as suggested and as I shuffled I saw her eying me with concern, so all I'd achieved by quizzing her was to make her believe I wasn't right in the head, due to sunstroke, caffeine poisoning or plain old insanity. On hearing clumsy movements indoors I made a desperate attempt to explain my choice of conversational topic.

"The truth is, Laura..." I began, before allowing my vocal chords to proceed as they saw fit. "... that when I met Hugo he told me that I might have to do any or all of the things I mentioned, so that's why I didn't take up his offer."

Laura's eyes goggled and her mouth fell open.

"I've been trying to sound you out on those terrible things to see how you felt about them in view of your friendship with Hugo. There, now I've told you," I concluded, before shrugging, slapping my thighs, and wondering just how wise my spontaneous speech had been.

"Oh, my goodness!" She turned to see Harry stepping through the French windows. "Oh, Harry, come and listen to this."

"What's up, love?" he said, lumbering over, grasping her shoulders and giving me the evil eye. "Has he been talking about stuff he shouldn't?"

"Yes... no, oh, he's just told me terrible things about Hugo. Tell him, Geoff."

In the meantime I'd run through the possible repercussions of my false revelation and was extremely relieved to find that I couldn't have said anything better even if I'd planned it.

"Hugo said I might be cigarette, people and arms smuggling, so I told him to go to hell," I said, a picture of righteousness. "As Laura's a good friend of his I felt that she just had to know what kind of person that man is."

"Too right. Belgian bastard. Oh, sorry, love. A bloke like that deserves to be... to be fed to the bloody pigs."

Maybe he will be one day, I thought but didn't say.

"Oh, it's just *too* awful," Laura wailed. "And I thought he was just a little bit naughty in his dealings. Cigarettes, well, that's not so bad, but *people* smuggling, and *weapons*! Drugs too, I imagine, the scoundrel."

"Yes, I expect so," I said.

"Oh, I shall never speak to him again as long as I live. Thank you for telling me, Geoff. You're a true friend."

"It's the least I could do, Laura, the least I could do. How about a beer, Harry?"

"How about several? Bloody hell, just imagine what you might have got yourself into," he said, before trudging back inside, shaking his head.

Out of the woods at last – for now there would be no trip to seek out the Belgian bounder – I felt the accumulated stress slip off my shoulders and looked forward to a good, therapeutic drink.

"Just one thing," came Harry's deep voice from the windows.

"Er, what?"

"Why didn't you tell us this straight away?"

"Well, I... oh, I see now that I should have, but I hated to break such bad news to Laura so soon after arriving."

"Hmm, yes, I see your point. If I ever found out that any pal of mine did stuff like that I'd soon sever all ties."

"Of course, I would too."

"After I'd thrashed the living daylights out of him for deceiving me, of course."

"Yes, me too, a sound thrashing," I said, my pores beginning to ease open in preparation for a cold sweat, but when I eyed Harry I saw a ruminative expression rather than the accusing or suspicious glare I'd feared, so I *was* out of the woods after all.

In the meantime Laura was prodding her mobile phone.

"There," she said. "That's Hugo's number gone. I wish I'd never met the swine now."

"We could report him to the police, you know," said Harry.

"Oh no, I might have to give evidence and I know nothing really," said Laura. "Let him dig his own grave."

"Yep, criminals always come to grief in the end. Now for those beers."

9

The following morning we set off shortly after sunrise and did a pleasantly undulating circular walk. Despite Harry's undiminished weightiness he had certainly become fitter since our arduous treks during our trip, and on cresting one especially steep rise I do declare that he got me ever so slightly out of puff, so I resolved to do plenty of strenuous hikes on my upcoming rug tour, during which I would visit all the villages on my hypothetical tour, thus converting it into a real one. I'd have to tell Harry and Laura that I was heading elsewhere, of course, and in a rare moment of gloom during our walk I foresaw myself touring perpetually for the rest of my life, always one step behind my real experiences, so I resolved to be deliberately vague about my future movements.

On returning to the house at about ten I was looking forward to diving into the pool – after showering first, of course – but on passing Bambi, Harry stopped to inspect her damaged posterior.

"Backed into summat, did you?"

"No, someone backed into me, in… Pizarra, outside a bakery. When I came out they'd buggered off. I'll get her fixed when I've got time."

"Let's have a look at these rugs then."

"Now?"

"No time like the present."

"I haven't got the key."

"Go and get it then."

I complied, opened the rather stiff door and invited them to feast their eyes on my stock.

Harry bounded inside and poked around for a while. "Hmm, plenty of colours to choose from, I'll say that," he said, before squeezing out again. "Take a peek, Laura."

One advantage of the reduced size and congested state of Bambi was that we could only go in one at a time, so when I saw Laura stiffen after stroking a few rugs I concluded that she didn't think much of my collection. The truth is that a quality rug can cost hundreds of pounds, and I wasn't so stupid as to believe that I'd got thirty first-rate items for two grand. As she fondled a few more I was pleased to see that Harry was looking elsewhere and taking the opportunity to scratch his crotch, so he didn't see her scratching her head and preparing, I knew, to give or conceal her verdict. When she turned to climb down, the first thing she saw was my half-resigned, half-imploring gaze, intended to transmit a desire not to be made a fool of in front of the merciless scoffer who had now taken off his t-shirt and was drying his armpits.

"Harry, please, our elderly Spanish neighbours won't wish to see you doing that," she said after looking at me in a half-complicit, half-pitying way.

"Sorry, love. What do you think of the rugs then?"

"They're very nice. Just the thing to sell in the villages, where people... er..." She frowned as she ground to a halt, but she'd done enough, bless her.

"... don't have much money," I said, taking the baton and running with it. "Yes, there's no point trying to sell really expensive ones to the locals, and it's them I want to deal with, as the rugs are mainly an excuse to meet people and have a good chat. Throughout history trade has brought different peoples together in a way that wouldn't have happened otherwise, leading to cultural as well as commercial exchange throughout the whole world. I mean, look at the Silk Road, Marco Polo and... the East India Company."

"All right, all right," said a reclothed Harry. "Your rugs aren't much cop, but you sell enough to get by. Not much future in that though, and you don't want to be spending that money you got off your aunt, do you?"

"No," I said, thinking about the six thousand-odd euros I had stashed in the space above the cab.

"What's that daft grin for? I'm serious, Geoff. Now that you've kicked that bastard Hugo into touch you've got to start thinking of a way to make real money. Hawking rugs is all very well, but if the cops catch you selling 'em they might confiscate the lot. Then where will you be, eh?"

"I know, Harry, and after the summer I'll look into doing something more lucrative," I said, picturing a snuffling pig, though I knew they used dogs, as Claudia had told me.

"I don't know," Laura chipped in. "This rug idea could be expanded upon. By buying from a wholesaler, using a bigger van and becoming self-employed I think it could become a viable enterprise. With quality rugs – I mean, even better ones than those – you'd only have to sell two or three a week to get by, and if you sold more you could make quite a lot of money. I think it's worth looking into."

I was thinking about driving a couple of hundred miles with a few boxes of truffles and receiving a big fat wad of cash at the end of it, but I just nodded and pursed my lips.

"We'll see," I said.

"Where are you heading next?" Harry asked.

"Well, I thought I'd drive to Coín and then check out the villages west from there," I said, because forewarned is forearmed and I'd already partially planned a route which I really might do, as they'd 'bought' my first route and I didn't want to play catch-up for the rest of my rug-selling life.

"Why not revisit the villages you've been to and try to build on that trade?" Harry asked, as I might have guessed he would.

"Oh, it's too soon for that," I said.

"I agree with Geoff," said my saviour. "Coín might be a bit too big, but there are lots of villages to the west. You might even get as far as Grazalema, which I believe you visited on your trip."

"Ah, yes, when Geoff did an extra-long walk while Jeremy and me bused it back," Harry said with a childish chuckle.

I laughed politely. "Don't remind me."

"So when will you set off?"

"Oh, there's no rush. He's only just arrived," said my kind hostess.

"The day after tomorrow, I think," I said, for despite having resolved the Hugo Problem, I had no wish to risk further grillings of any kind, and the truth was that I rather fancied touring the sierra and getting shut of a few rugs, having already visualised the experience so thoroughly.

"So you'll reach Coín by Tuesday evening?"

"Yes, well, somewhere near there where I can camp."

"Nah, you can stay with us."

"No, I'd better get back on the road and shift a few rugs."

"I mean you can stay at the hotel with us. We're coming with you."

"What?"

"You OK with that, Laura?"

"Yes, I don't see why not, for a couple of days at least," said his compliant partner.

"That'll be long enough to set him on the right track," Harry said, grasping my shoulder with his sweaty paw. "Come on, let's have a dip before lunch."

***

Coín is a sizeable town about twenty miles to the west of Malaga and though it was pleasant to stay in a decent hotel for once, I didn't relish what awaited me the following day. Over an excellent dinner – which they wouldn't let me pay for due to my supposed poverty – Harry waxed lyrical about his proposed tactics for the morrow, when he intended to mastermind a two-pronged attack in the biggish village of Guaro, a few miles to the west.

"You've got to target the foreigners too, Geoff," he said, waving a greasy fork at me. "Stands to reason, as they've got more cash and they're always buying stuff because they've got sod all else to do."

Like you, I thought. "I suppose so," I said.

"So, what we do is this. While you pull your usual stunt with the locals, Laura and me will sniff out any foreigners and engage them in conversation; me if they're Brits, and Laura if they're continentals, because they'll understand her better. What we *must* avoid though, is converging on Bambi at the same time. I mean, we don't want an old dear being barged aside by some great German lump, do we?"

"No," I said, though I doubted there'd be much converging going on. As I'd described my previous, purely fictional, rug-selling sprees in such vivid detail, they really believed it was possible to cajole people over to a dented old van to see a load of cheap rugs and then, on top of that, actually buy one. I was nervous enough about my part of Harry's plan, as it would be no easy chore to prise morning punters off their bar stools to look at something they had no interest it, but to have Harry stomping around the place hassling everyone in shorts only added to my impending woes. Harry had sold little in his life, but when he had occasionally wished to shift a superfluous item – like an old TV, child's bike, or fishing rod – there was no peace in the local pub until someone had succumbed, usually just to get him off their back, sometimes literally, as he could be a very tactile merchant when push came to shove, as it often did, and once the TV/bike/rod had been unloaded there was a collective sigh of relief as the great lummox returned to his serene, beer-guzzling ways.

"Harry, dear, I'm not sure the foreigners will be interested in Geoff's current stock of rugs," said Laura, who was as uneasy as I was about our unenviable task. "They're very nice and colourful, but… er, affluent people may not wish to buy them. Also, though Bambi is a sweet little van, her appearance might not instil confidence in potential buyers. I think Geoff's opportunistic tactic is more viable; you know, just chat to people in the bar, who may be a little tipsy, and eventually find a … what's the word?"

"Sucker," I said.

"Well, yes, that's one way of putting it."

"Pah! Geoff has to think *big* if he wants to make some serious cash. Oh, ye of little faith!" He stroked Laura's arm with his right hand and squeezed my shoulder with his left. "Tomorrow you'll see."

"Maybe," said Laura.

"Ouch," said I.

"Sorry," said Harry, allowing my clavicle to unbend. "A quick brandy and then off to bed, eh?"

***

By the time I reached the village square in Guaro the following morning, Harry had already dropped Laura off at a café – for she was feeling unwell, the crafty lass – and was lamenting the fact that bollards prevented me from parking in the tiny plaza, so he jumped in beside me and we managed to park, very badly, on a nearby street. On walking back to the square we saw little activity, for it was only eight o'clock, which prompted me to make the following unfortunate comment.

"I didn't imagine it'd be like this."

"What do you mean, you didn't *imagine* it'd be like this?"

I engaged my sleepy brain. "This place, I mean. Most of the other places I visited were smaller and the square was the focal point of the village, and there weren't any of these stupid bollards," I said, glad that the shrewd Laura was feigning illness. "I'd drive into the spacious plaza where the locals would be going about their business and all eyes would turn to Bambi. Their curiosity aroused, once I began to chat it was a cinch to get them to wander over to take a peek, whereupon more folk would cluster around and I'd give them my rug spiel. I can't see how we'll manage that in this higgledy-piggledy place."

"Hmm, I see what you mean. What we want is a smaller, woolly-back kind of place where they're bored to death of seeing each other. We're too close to the coast here and I can't see any gormless punters right now. I can't see anyone, in fact, except that postman over there."

"I'm sure you're right. I reckon I ought to head off inland and check out the tiny villages... like I did before." I held out my hand. "Thanks anyway, Harry. I'll see you in a couple of weeks, once I've sold this load of rugs."

Harry gazed at my open hand and scratched his head. "Wait there," he said, and was off, so I lowered my hand and watched him stomp away across the square, only to return a few minutes later.

"Sorted. Let's go," he said, before heading towards Bambi with a disturbingly purposeful stride.

I caught him up. "Where are we going?"

"To the nearest little village. Laura's going to drive back to Coín and wait for us at the hotel. Her head's aching like mad, poor thing."

"Maybe you should go with her. I'm sure I'll man—"

"Just one village. I'll watch you in action, give you a few tips, then you drive me back and shoot off again tomorrow."

Another night in a wide bed was a comforting thought, so though dismayed by Harry's pathological persistence I consoled myself with the fact that in twenty-four hours I'd be a free man once more.

A little over half an hour later we trundled into the hamlet of Jorox, perched on the green mountainside and every bit as tiny and isolated as Harry had desired: more so, in fact, as there were hardly any houses at all. There was a bar, however, overlooking a street on which half a dozen vehicles were parked, so my guide and tutor decided that it was as good a place as any to start.

"But there's hardly anyone here," I protested.

"It's either here or back to that Alozaina place we just passed, which looked as big as Guaro. I don't want to leave Laura alone for too long, so take your pick."

I glanced at the motley assortment of vehicles and heard loud chatter from the bar. Fearing that my embarrassment would only be multiplied in a larger place, I consented to give it a go.

"How's your Spanish, Harry? Judging by the cars and vans they must be locals."

"It's coming along, thanks to Laura, but you'll find that the universal language of barter will do nicely," he said, before yanking open Bambi's back door and dragging out a couple of rugs, which he deftly shouldered and set off up the slope. Slipping easily into my role of disciple, and even beginning to relish the thought of Harry making a first-class fool of himself, I politely ushered him through the door and noted the sudden silence within.

He dumped the rugs on a table by the door, before briefly greeting the assembled yokels and ordering two beers from the dozy young waiter. Half past nine was a little early for me, but when he then requested, quite competently, two bocadillos of sausage, bacon and black pudding, I realised that we were having a second breakfast, the one at the hotel having been rather meagre due to the early hour of our departure.

"Doubt they'll speak our lingo, but talk broad just in case," he said in a strong Lancashire accent.

"Reight. What's plan, like?"

"Nowt fer now. Get that down yer and keep 'em guessin'. Fat feller's gawpin' at rugs already."

"Aye, he is that," I said, for though I speak the Queen's English as well as the next cultured man, I wasn't averse to a spot of vernacular from time to time.

"Old skinny un wi't glass eye's lookin' o'er too," Harry mumbled with a mouthful of butty. 'Nother ale?"

"Aye, ger 'em in. Young specky-four-eyed git's wandrin' o'er t' rugs." I craned my neck. "Ee'll be mitherin' us in a mo'."

"Head down and scoff yer grub, lad. Mek 'em wait. Reight laugh this, i'nt it?"

"Aye, oo' der thought wi'd be doin' this? Did yer plan it, like?"

"Nay, just nouse. Now t'bar chap's tekin' a look. When he comes back order two more in yer best Spanish."

On requesting two more glasses of beer in fluent Andaluz, the waiter's shifty eyes opened a tad wider and he inquired as to why the rugs were occupying a table.

"Just airing them. We've a vanful, you see," I said, before eying Harry.

"Ball's in your court now, lad, so work yer magic on 'im."

I breathed deeply in and out of my nostrils, as is my wont before a creative outpouring. "We've got thirty top quality rugs from Morocco in the van that we're taking to a souvenir shop in… Ronda. They expect them to be in excellent condition, so whenever we stop we air a couple."

The boy's brow crinkled and his lower jaw dangled.

"It's the silk in them, you see. It needs to breathe."

"Heavy in van though," said Harry in pidgin Spanish. "If we sell few, better for us."

"By 'eck, lad, tha's picked a bit of Spanish up," I said.

"Aye, grand teacher Laura is, to ger it into this thick 'ead o' mine, eh?"

"Aye. What'll I tell 'im now?"

"Ger 'im out t'van. Tuthers'll follow. Gormless wazzocks 'ave nowt better to do."

I cleared my throat. "Yes, we wouldn't mind selling a few of the less expensive ones to lessen our load. Come and have a look."

The lad shrugged, lifted the bar flap and followed me outside. Five more fellows of assorted shapes, sizes and ages tagged along, while Harry brought up the rear like an unusually well-nourished shepherd.

So, for the first time ever I displayed Bambi's wares on the street, though I had an uncannily *déjà vu* feeling, I must say. The motley crew shuffled, pawed and mumbled, but when I was about to launch into my first ever sales pitch, Harry put his finger to his lips.

"Let 'em gawp. Look at scenery and say nowt fer now."

I leant lightly on the railings and gazed down into the valley until a while later a finger prodded my shoulder. The owner of the finger proved to be a short, portly chap of sixty whose neat clothing suggested he might well be the owner of the shiny Seat Leon, the only vehicle within sight to have been built this century.

"How much for that one?" he asked, pointing to a shaggy blue, green, orange, yellow and white number measuring about four feet by three.

I looked at Harry.

"Cuatrocientos (400)," he said calmly.

"Qué?!" exclaimed the man.

"Tell 'im why," Harry said.

"Er, the rug you have indicated is our finest, made my Tuareg tribeswomen in a remote village of the Atlas Mountains – by hand, of course – and conveyed to the coast by camel."

The man chortled, then spat over the railings. "I'll give you eighty for it."

"The rug is woven of the finest silk, wool and… camel h–"

"Leave 'im to me now, lad," said Harry. "Trescientos," he said to the man.

"Eighty-five," he countered.

Thus ensued a tremendous bout of haggling between Harry and the stubborn chap, while the rest of us looked on, me with bated breath and the others with varying degrees of amusement. After a hard-fought battle of wits the man handed over €140 and shook both our hands, a look of triumph in his avaricious eyes. His pals were quietly jubilant and as we trooped back into the bar I felt pretty hard done by, until Harry put my mind at ease over coffee and brandy.

"Listen, you chump, four hundred was a crazy price."

"I'd begun to believe it was worth it. I'd begun to believe it really was made of silk, wool and… stuff. As the price came down I thought my heart would break."

"Ha, the only beast that pile of crap's seen is the great big machine it came out of. Artificial fibres through and through."

"Really?"

"Yep, you can tell by the touch. You've just got a bloody good deal and you're paying for breakfast."

"Gladly. Thanks, Harry."

"Got the idea now?"

"Yes, I think so. I'll add your method to my repertoire of… methods."

"Do that. When I see you next I expect to see a rug-free zone in the back of Bambi and at *least* a couple of grand in your pocket."

"Right," I said, sure that I could fulfil both those objectives, one way or another. "But I have to drive you back to Coín yet."

"Nah, drop me on the main road. I'll stroll along for a while, maybe hitch to Guaro, and then get Laura to pick me up. Ha, her headache'll have gone by now, I'm sure. I don't think she fancied rug selling. She's a bit too refined for that sort of thing, I reckon."

So it was that I soon found myself alone once more, trundling towards Ronda on a road that I recognised from our previous trip. Keen to follow up on my recent success, for I was sure that my smooth patter had clinched the deal, I scanned the map in search of a similarly godforsaken place and ended up heading north along a minor road to a small village called Serrato. It was a neat little place with several streets, but so isolated that I felt sure my rugs would delight the locals, deprived as they were of all but the most rudimentary shops. Once again my idyllic village square failed to materialise, but there was a raised mini-plaza containing a bar, so I decided to flog a rug or two before moving on for a late lunch elsewhere, our hearty breakfast having sated me for the time being. Deciding to replicate my previous sale insomuch as I was able, I selected a pair of colourful rugs and lugged them up some steps to the bar, where I pushed open the door with my foot and proceeded to unload them onto a table, just as Harry had done.

"Hey, what do you think you're doing?" the presumed owner – a thickset man of forty with fiery eyes, a bulbous nose and a thick-lipped, scowling mouth – called from behind the bar.

"Er, just leaving them here for a moment while I take coffee," I replied, the soul of civility.

He grunted. "No selling in here, or anywhere else in the village, except on market day."

"Which is?"

"Not today. What can I get you?"

"Un cortado, por favor." I hopped onto a stool and surveyed the other customers, all men, none of whom had shown the slightest interest in me or my rugs. While sipping my coffee and rueing my bad luck, a dapper old chap slid onto the stool beside me and was silently served a glass of wine.

"From Morocco, are you?" he said.

"No, what makes you say that?"

"Oh, the rugs, the knackered van outside. Bound to be one of them, I thought, but I see now that you're not."

Although I was as tanned as many Moroccans, I wasn't pleased to be mistaken for one, not because I have anything against North Africans, far from it, but because I knew they were held in low esteem in Spain, especially in backward, one-horse backwaters like this one.

"I am British, and proud of it," I replied with a haughty sneer.

"I see. Fallen on hard times, have you?"

"No, I have *not*, sir. I am merely spending the summer touring around for my health and, while I'm at it, offloading a few rugs for a friend of mine."

"Oy! I told you, no selling," said the dratted ogre behind the bar.

"I am *not* selling, but merely conversing with this gentleman," I said through gritted teeth, before turning to my companion. "Is this how he treats all newcomers to his dingy bar, the great oaf?" I murmured.

"Oh, he's not a bad man when you get to know him," he said with a chuckle.

"I wish I'd never entered this flea-infested hole. A curse on the racist swine and all others of his ilk," I said, seething by now.

"It isn't a bad little bar, you know," said the old gent, his cursed chuckling riling me further, for a man with several thousand euros to his name and the means to make a minor fortune once the Italian truffle season commenced had no need to endure insults from a thick hick of a bar owner, so I told him so, omitting to mention the truffles, of course.

The old chap chuckled some more. "Paco, come here," he said to the object of my scorn.

He came. "Sí, papá?"

As the more competent linguists among my readers will know, papá means dad, or daddy, in Spanish, so I awaited the father-son exchange with some trepidation, the younger man not being someone I wished to grapple with just then, as the sausage, bacon and black pudding I'd scoffed were sitting heavily on my far from settled stomach.

"Son, has Sandra cleaned the bar this morning?" he asked.

"Of course, as always. Why do you ask, papá?"

I finished my coffee.

"Oh, because our friend here has his doubts."

I fished a euro coin from my pocket and slid it onto the bar.

"Doubts about what, papá?"

"Adiós," I muttered, stepping down from my stool.

"About the cleanliness of our establishment."

I shuffled away slowly, maintaining my poise.

"And he thinks very little of you, son."

I began to gather up the rugs.

"And called you an oaf and a racist swine, I seem to recall."

"Oy!" the offended party yelled, before vaulting the bar with surprising agility.

In my haste to avoid an altercation which might have forced me to defend myself with some vigour, for I felt sure that the bull-like fellow was in no mood to parley, I was forced to abandon one of my rugs, leave the bar and trot down the steps with the other, which I quickly bundled into Bambi, before hopping into the cab and starting her up. As I began to pull away, already regretting not having taught the brute a lesson, a tremendous thud on the roof made me accelerate with skilful smoothness, for if it was the rug up there I didn't want to lose it, and if it was the brute there'd be time enough to hurl him off on a handy bend. By the time I reached the main road I'd heard no noise from above, so I stopped, hopped out, retrieved my now dangling rug, shoved it in the back and drove on.

After a while I began to see the funny side of things and laughed heartily as I motored down the main road to Ronda. Good heavens, I thought as I giggled and guffawed happily along, how on earth did a man of my calibre get himself into such a senselessly silly situation? Why was I maintaining this façade of peddling rugs to peasants when I could live the good life until Claudia called me? After all, now that I'd sold a rug at a handsome profit, what more did I need to prove? Bambi was ever so cramped in the back too, so when I'd wiped away my tears of laughter I decided to head straight to Ronda and sell my whole stock to a shop, apart from a red, brown, yellow and violet number which I'd grown to like and fancied lying upon when lounging by the van.

Conscious of the fact that the cultivated reader can only stomach so many scenes of a commercial nature, I won't subject you to a detailed account of how I got shut of my unwanted rugs, save to say that after visiting several souvenir shops in that touristy place I eventually sold the lot, apart from the one I mentioned, to two Moroccan gentlemen in a Transit van. I'd spotted the two dusky immigrants after being harried out of a bike shop which I'd entered on the off chance, or rather they had spotted me, as one of them asked me why I was carting rugs around in the heat of the day. While apprising them of my unwelcome burden it occurred to me that it was about time I did a good deed, not having done one for a while, and I realised that by selling them the rugs cheaply I could ameliorate their hand-to-mouth existence in an instant, so after a little gentle, purely symbolic bargaining I agreed to sell them for a mere €600, upon which the older of the two whipped out a wad of notes and peeled off twelve fifties.

"How will you dispose of the rugs, my friends?" I asked them after shaking their toilworn hands.

"We have a market stall here on Sundays," said the younger man.

"That's good."

"Other days we go to markets on the coast. The foreigners will like these rugs," said the older man.

"Well I hope you make a jolly good profit."

"Oh, we will," the younger man said with a gleam of gratitude in his careworn eyes.

After helping them to transfer the merchandise to their van, I gave my living quarters a good dust with an old pair of boxer shorts, before lying down on the left-hand bed and luxuriating in Bambi's spaciousness, because quite frankly the rugs had been a royal pain in the neck, but they'd helped me out of a tight spot, so my slight loss was outweighed by the fact that I could now reveal some of my stash to Harry – maybe three grand – and bask in my supposed success, before informing him that my rug selling days were over.

'So what will you do now?' his booming voice would say, and as I was loath to invent another spurious scheme I resolved to stay out of his way for a while, as another interrogation was the last thing I needed, especially if Laura relented and decided to call Hugo, or if he called her, a possibility that occurred to me then for the first time, but which I dismissed from my mind as being simply too awful to contemplate. I opened my map and scanned the coast, as the hilly interior had been all very well for a while, but by then I was pining for the seaside once more.

10

To cut a long story a little shorter, for there is still much to tell, I repaired to the coastal village of La Mamola, about sixty miles east of Torre del Mar, and rented a modest apartment for a month in order to avoid the August heat and live tranquilly between brick walls for a while before my arduous truffle trips began. La Mamola is a small but cosmopolitan place, due mainly to the many square miles of plastic stretched over the nearby fields, under which workers from many countries labour to produce the fruit and veg that all of us enjoy. As a consequence La Mamola wasn't overburdened with tourists, though there were some, as the narrow beach is passably sandy, but as I was in Spain to work, on the whole I preferred to rub shoulders with fellow toilers than idling sun-worshippers.

It was after I'd spent about a week in my rather spartan little pad – waiting in vain for Claudia to call – that I met Alina, a gorgeous Romanian girl who was fortunate enough not to have to work in the searing heat of the hothouses. Her family was wealthy, she told me soon after we'd met one evening while strolling along the front, so unlike her compatriots, of whom there were many, she spent her days studying for the law degree which she would complete the following year in Madrid.

"So why are you here, Alina, dear? La Mamola isn't the chicest spot on the coast, after all."

"True, Geoff, but I prefer to stay here with my honest, hardworking countrymen than live it up in Marbella, where my sister, a concert pianist, now resides in the family apartment," she said in her excellent Spanish.

After we'd sauntered up and down for a while she suggested a spot of dinner, so we entered the nearest restaurant, called Casa Patricio, and gorged ourselves on fresh seafood, washed down with the best white wine that money could buy. I winced as I paid the bill, but it had been worth it, because in that short space of time I had become quite intimate with that tall, slim, blonde beauty who remarked that though I was considerably older than her, I looked and talked like a much younger man.

"Everyone says that," I said, reaching over to stroke her hand, having already cleaned mine in the little bowl provided.

"It's so good to meet a man of culture and knowledge," she said with a sigh. "My compatriots are good people, but not worldly like you."

"Ha, that's one advantage of my forty-something years," I said, for she'd already taken ten years off me. "One lives and learns," I added, before filling her in on the salient points of my rollercoaster life, omitting to mention the smuggling and the rugs, of course.

She listened with glistening eyes and astonished sighs, and when a tough-looking pal of hers popped in to see her, she ushered him away with a dreamy smile.

"He's not your boyfriend, is he?" I asked with a chuckle.

"Oh, no, Razvan's just a friend. He's a little overprotective at times, but his heart's in the right place."

"Does he work under that infernal plastic?"

"What? Oh no, he's on holiday too. He owns a gym in… Torremolinos."

Anyway, one thing led to another and, as you might have guessed, it wasn't difficult to lure her back to my pad, and I will employ a series of dots …… rather than describe the passionate night that followed, as this is a book for all age groups and persuasions. I must say it was extremely pleasant to frolic between the sheets with that feisty piece, as what with one thing and another it had been quite a while since I'd had the opportunity to do what I do best, and after our third bout of ……, before which she had …… me … for the first time, she swore that she'd learnt more in one night than in two years with her first and only former boyfriend, a highly rated Romanian novelist. I must say that her passionate sighs, squeals, moans and occasional howls suggested that I'd lost none of my prowess in the sack, and I do declare that the image of Claudia faded from my mind for the first time in ages.

The following morning, after treating her to a wholesome, restorative breakfast, I offered to walk her back to the apartment she shared with a female medical student, but she declined my offer, planted one final kiss on my tender lips and swayed away on her rather incongruous high heels, which she'd soon be kicking off before getting down to her day's studies. Our seafood dinners and subsequent sensual and mostly sleepless nights became a regular occurrence, and though on the first weekend she had to go Barcelona to see her father, a surgeon, on the second we drove down to Malaga in her friend's BMW, for she hadn't been at all taken by Bambi when I showed her to her, and had become quite glum for a while afterwards.

She soon cheered up in Malaga, however, as we stayed at the posh parador hotel overlooking the bay and I wined and dined her as only I know how, as well as taking her on a shopping spree along the boulevards, for it turned out that her handsome trimonthly allowance had been delayed, leaving her in a bit of a spot, so I didn't hesitate to hand her a couple of hundred now and then, as what is money for if not to spend? One week drifted seamlessly into another and our pleasant routine of eating, drinking, strolling, shopping and sexual gymnastics – for she was a fast learner – made for a sublimely pleasant interlude, though I must say that my munificence made quite a hole in my stash of cash, so much so that by the first Friday in September I had to insist that we stay in the village rather than drive down the coast, as our visits to the Torrequebrada casino had proven especially hard on the pocket.

"I shall go anyway," she said to my surprise.

"Without me, sweetie?"

"Yes," she said with a frown I hadn't seen since showing her Bambi.

"Until Monday evening then. We could eat a pizza for a change," I said, as her insatiable appetite for seafood had made me detest the stuff.

"Yes. Adiós, Geoff," she said, planting a rather dry kiss on my lips.

"Au revoir, you mean, babe."

"As you like," she said, and was gone – never to return, it turned out – and nor did I see her annoyingly ubiquitous pal Razvan again either, so I assume he drove the ungrateful wench back to Madrid to commence her studies.

Feeling drained both physically and financially by our month of passion I spent an extremely quiet week in my apartment, resting and repeatedly counting my money which, try as I might, never added up to more than €132.15, so you can imagine the elation I felt when Claudia called one morning while I was languishing in bed, feeling just a tad sorry for myself on finally realising that Alina had taken me for a ride in more ways than one, though I had a few photos to console me and to show Harry to prove that I'd bedded a real beauty.

"Claudia, darling! What took you so long?" I said, beside myself with joy on hearing her dulcet tones.

"Hi, Geoff, I'm sorry I couldn't call earlier, but I've been ever so busy."

"Doing what, may I ask?"

"Oh, preparing Project T."

"Be careful what you say on the phone," I warned her, for though I was delighted to hear her for personal reasons – Alina having merely whetted my appetite – my brain had immediately clicked back into business mode.

"It's OK. It's a payphone."

Drat, I thought, will I *never* get her phone number?

"Very sensible, dear," I said. "When do we meet?"

"We don't, I'm afraid, not yet anyway. I have a date for your next assignment."

"Great," I said, for I knew that €132.15 wouldn't last forever, despite having stocked up on tinned food, long-life milk and the utterly tasteless sliced bread they sell in Spain.

"Do you have a pen and paper?"

"Yes, somewhere in my suite. Just a moment. OK, fire away."

"Next Thursday, the 15th of September, you are to drive to the Cabo de Gata."

"I know it."

"To a little place called La Isleta del Moro, between San José and Las Negras."

"I know Las Negras. That's where we met Laura."

"Oh, yes, I remember."

"Er, I don't suppose Hugo's heard from her, has he?" I said calmly while tapping frantically on the table.

"I don't think so. What's that noise?"

"Oh, something outside the hotel. Are you not going to ask me where I am or what I've been doing, love?"

"Not now, Geoff. So…"

"So you're not sure if Hugo's heard from Laura then?"

"Does it matter?"

"No… well, yes."

"You haven't told her anything, have you?"

"Of course not, but it's in our interests for them not to speak, isn't it?"

"All right then, I'm *sure* he hasn't contacted her. Satisfied?"

"Immensely. Now, do go on."

"On reaching the first buildings of La Isleta del Moro, after approaching from Las Negras, you will turn left and enter the beach parking area. There you will leave your van in a discrete place at exactly 0100, place the key under the mat and walk into the village, as there is little cover near the beach. There will be nothing open at that time, so you must sit on a bench somewhere and contemplate the sea. If anyone approaches you, pretend you are drunk or something, but don't engage them in conversation. At exactly 0230 hours you walk casually back to the van, which will be in the same place. Shall I repeat that?"

"No, I have it."

"Right, retrieve the key and drive back the way you came. You are to join the A-7 motorway beyond Campohermoso and drive up to Cartagena."

"Ah, a city I've always meant to visit."

"The total distance is 175 kilometres, so in that van of yours you can expect to arrive at about 0530 hours."

"No problem. Now I've sold all my rugs she goes like the clappers."

"Ah, the rugs, yes. So, once in Cartagena you are to go to an area called Lo Campano, to the south-east of the city centre."

"Got it."

"*How* can you have got it, Geoff? Do you have a street plan of Cartagena open in front of you?"

"Er, no, but I can ask."

"You *cannot* ask, you... silly boy."

"I like it when you call me a silly boy," I said in the sexy voice that I'd often employed with Alina when urging her to .. .... on me one more time.

"So, just before you arrive in Lo Campano from the direction of the city you will see a Repsol petrol station, which will be closed. You will leave the van behind the building and walk back towards the city centre."

"After leaving the key under the mat?"

"Yes. On no account walk into Lo Campano itself, as it's a very... unwholesome place and you might be mugged."

"I can take care of myself, babe."

"You won't *need* to take care of yourself, as you're not to set foot in the place, understand?"

"Yes."

"Just walk purposefully towards the city, as if you're going to work or something, and time it so you get back at 0630. Then you–"

"Retrieve the key, check the envelopes are there and drive away, right?"

"Right, but there'll be just one envelope, for you."

"A fat one?"

"Fairly. On this first assignment you may notice that the weight of the goods is not heavy."

"I guess tru... the goods are pretty light but bulky, eh?"

"Yes, or rather no. Oh, as you won't be able to resist looking I might as well tell you that you'll be carrying just three boxes of top quality truffles."

"Shush!"

"I'm still on a payphone. This first run is something of a trial. If it goes well we'll be carrying more truffles next time, so you'll earn more. Now, if you have to look up Lo Campano on your phone, do so, but please clear the search history afterwards. Do you know how to do that?"

"But of course."

"Good, it's just that some older people don't... anyway. Oh, do you still have credit on the phone?"

"Yes," I said with total certainty, as during over two months in Spain I'd called no-one and only Harry had called me. I'd expected a friendly call from Jeremy, to see how I was getting on, but as he hadn't called, neither had I, as I felt that being the traveller *I* deserved a call, rather than the other way round.

"Geoff, are you still there?"

"Present and correct."

"What?"

"Yes, I'm still here."

"Right, also remember to destroy the notes you've just made before you set off."

"Ha, I've been eating plenty of fish, so my memory's in tiptop shape," I said, though by now I was down to tinned tuna thanks to that Romanian gold-digger. "When will you call me, Claudia?"

"The day after the job."

"And then we'll meet?"

"Probably, yes. Goodbye then, and good luck."

"Farewell my lovely, and don't worry, as the truffles will be safe with me," I said, before snorting, kissing the mouthpiece, hanging up and dashing off to a bar to have a decent meal, now that my money worries would soon be over.

**

At midday on the 14th I left my apartment and drove the eighty miles to Campohermoso, where I had a snooze and killed some time drinking coffee in the bars, so when I set off to my final destination I was as alert as an eagle and also quite curious to see the arrival of the truffle craft, but as the area around the beach was indeed very bare, I obeyed my instruction to the letter and strolled into the village. There I found a little concrete-covered jetty from where I could make out bobbing boats on the calm moonlit sea, so I settled down to wait. A headland blocked my view of the beach, however, so when I walked back to Bambi it was with some trepidation, as had the truffles not arrived I would soon be in serious financial difficulty, being down to my last €71.45. I rued the fact that I'd left my favourite rug in the apartment in lieu of two weeks' outstanding rent, for though Alina and I had frolicked upon it, just for a change, it would still have fetched a bob or two.

On feeling for the key under the mat I knew it had been used and replaced, and when I shone my handy little torch into the back I saw three boxes in the aisle, just as Claudia had promised. Preferring to sate my curiosity sooner rather than later, I nipped round and hopped inside, and on prodding a box I found it to be much heavier than expected, though to be honest I had no idea how much real truffles weighed, only ever having eaten the chocolate variety. All three boxes were equally weighty, so I deduced that they must have compressed the stuff, and in the wink of an eye I was back on the road. Only two and a half hours later I arrived in the coastal city of Cartagena and found my way to Lo Campano without difficulty, having memorised the route thoroughly, but as I was a bit early I decided to drive past the petrol station and take a peek at the place that Claudia had considered so unwholesome. It was certainly a dump, I reflected as I toured the shabby streets of crumbling buildings with a few burnt-out cars dotted around, and I wondered why she had chosen such a rough place in which to hand over a product destined for the finest restaurants in Spain, but it wasn't mine to reason why, so I returned to the garage, parked up behind it, left the key under the mat and walked back towards the city.

After about ten minutes I reached a decent neighbourhood and on hearing a metal shutter roll up I beheld a well-lit bar about to commence its day's business, so rather than wandering around aimlessly for half an hour I popped in and ordered a coffee.

"Early start today, eh?" said the chubby-cheeked young chap, who seemed in remarkably good spirits considering the time, 0557 hours, to be precise.

"Yes, I've just made a delivery."

"Ah, and off back to Britain now, are you?"

"What makes you say that?"

"Oh, I studied there last summer, in Brighton, so I recognised the accent."

A little miffed by this, I concluded that my month spent conversing with a foreigner had taken the edge off my Andaluz drawl, but he was such a cheerful lad that I admitted that I was from Lancaster in the north of England.

"I might go to the north next year. I hate this dump of a city and I like to go abroad whenever I can."

"Speaking of dumps, what do you think of Lo Campano," I asked out of idle curiosity.

His benign face clouded. "Nobody goes there."

"But it's very near."

"Yes, but it's like another world. Even the police don't go there if they can help it."

"Oh, I've parked my… truck behind the petrol station there."

"Hmm, it should be OK for now, but don't leave it too long. Ha, by the time you get back you'll probably see a couple of scruffy guys standing around on the pavement in front of the forecourt. Do you know what they'll be doing?"

"Er, no."

"They're there to watch out for the police. If a couple of cop cars go past, as there's never just one, they make calls to warn folk to hide their stuff."

"What stuff?"

"Oh, drugs and guns, but mainly drugs. Didn't you know that people come from miles around to score there?"

"No, I didn't."

"I'm surprised you've made a delivery anywhere near the place. What do you carry?"

"Er… foodstuff."

"Hmm, very odd. When you get back you want to ask your boss why they deliver there. Sounds a bit fishy to me."

"Me too. Tell me, in this Lo Campano place do they also deal in truffles?"

"What?"

"Truffles. You know, the things that pigs sniff out, though they use dogs nowadays as they don't eat the stuff."

"Ha, I can't imagine those dirty gypsy bastards having anything to do with truffles."

Ignoring his deplorable xenophobia I remarked that white Italian truffles were the finest in the world and fetched a hefty price on the black market, to which he merely shrugged and remarked that if there was money in it, they'd try anything rather than put in an honest day's work. So, though I regretted my impulsive outburst, I'd learnt that it *was* plausible that they'd branched out into truffles, though I'd certainly be having words with Claudia about Hugo's dubious choice of handover location. I finished my coffee, bid him good day and hurried back to Bambi, fearing that she might have been stolen by some passing travellers keen to add to their fleet. The petrol station had opened and, sure enough, there were two dishevelled young fellows smoking roll-up cigarettes out front, but after checking that the boxes had gone I lost no time in clearing out of there and I didn't stop to inspect my envelope until I'd left the motorway at a little place called Las Palas, some fifteen miles to the west of the city.

After parking on the main street of the sleepy little village I climbed into the back and thrust my hand under the left-hand cushions, where I found nothing, but before my sweat glands could muster themselves I tried the other bed and felt the magical touch of brown paper, though I wasn't sure it was brown until I'd pulled it out, but it was, and within the envelope I found a grand total of five thousand euros (€5000), consisting of one hundred used fifty euro notes. As you can imagine, my feeling of joy and relief was considerable, as I was once more in the pink after my draining month with that insatiable Romanian sow, and as I sank down on the left-hand bed for a well-earned nap I reflected that the world of truffles was a new and mysterious one for me and that no doubt Claudia would have a good reason for having sent me to such an unmitigated hellhole.

On awakening at two in the afternoon I found that my subconscious had been buzzing merrily away and had concluded that the fishiness of my mission was undeniable and that I would have to give Claudia a gruelling grilling when she called me the following day. After a spot of lunch I hastened back towards Malaga and spent the night at a luxury hotel near the beach in Torrox Costa, only a dozen miles short of Torre del Mar, a place

I'd become rather bored of by then, having stayed at two campsites – nudist and semi-clothed – and visited many of the bars and restaurants. Torrox Costa – not to be confused with Torrox town, though it's practically the same place – is an agreeable resort, especially in September when the hordes of hedonistic holidaymakers have departed, and it was my intention to lure Claudia there and have it out with her, not only about my professional misgivings, but also regarding our simmering but yet to be consummated relationship.

The last time I'd seen her, outside Hugo's house, we'd become tenderly tactile for the first time – if you don't count the punch on the nose, which I don't – so after clearing up the Lo Campano paradox I intended to whisk her off her feet and into my bed, for if nothing else Alina had run me in thoroughly and I was longing to resume my libidinous ways, after which I might or might not propose marriage, as although still young at heart it was about time I settled down and set about continuing the Corless line, though my wild oats might well have produced a few little Geoffs and Geoffesses over the years, as I wasn't always as careful as I was with Alina, who insisted on me using a …… every time.

The following morning I was lounging by the huge hotel pool when the phone finally rang.

"Claudia!" I exclaimed.

"You what?" said Harry.

"Harry," I murmured.

"Who's Claudia?"

"Oh, just a bird I met. How's it going?"

"We're fine. So?"

"So what?" I said, trying frantically to erase the last six weeks from my memory and replace them with rug-related endeavours.

"How've you been getting on? We thought you were coming back here. It was Laura who insisted I ring you, as I was in no hurry to talk to you," he said in his deadpan way.

"Ha, nice one. Well, I've been selling rugs."

"Where?"

"All over the place."

"Like where?"

"Well, when I left you I headed gradually north, then east, then south… to Granada to buy some more," I said, the old neurones gradually coming to life. "Then I drove through the Alpujarras. You know, where we went on the trip."

"Yes."

"I went to Órgiva, Pampaneira, Capileira, Trevélez–"

"Yes, Geoff, I remember the names too. How many have you sold?"

"Well…all in all, about… forty."

"That's great. And how much have you made?"

"Well, in total, about… five grand," I said, thanking my lucky stars that he hadn't called when I'd been practically down and out in La Mamola after Alina had sucked me dry and buggered off.

"Not bad, not bad. So who's this Claudia bird then?"

Having Alina fresh in my mind, I instantly transposed our fling, with modifications, and told him that I'd been holed up in La Mamola for a week with a Brazilian belle called Claudia, who I'd finally given the boot before relocating to Torrox.

"Brazilian, eh? Wonder what she was doing there. Ha, not a prossie, I hope."

"Come on, Harry, I'm not so dumb as to waste my money on whores. No, she's a law student, just twenty-three, and she will insist on calling me, despite the fact that I've kicked her into touch."

"Interesting."

"Is it?"

"Yes, because you sounded bloody pleased to hear from her until you realised it was me."

"Oh, well, I'm…. letting her down gently, you see, as I don't want to upset her."

"Bullshit, but never mind. The main reason I'm calling is because Jeremy and June are coming out a week from now. They'll be staying with us for a fortnight, so get your arse up here at some point."

"Brilliant, yes, I will."

"You never know, they might buy a rug off you," he said with an uncouth cackle.

I clicked my fingers, told the hovering waiter I desired nothing, and prepared to round off my rug enterprise with a mendacious flourish.

"The truth is, Harry, that I'm just about rugged out now."

"Don't talk like a bloody teenager."

"Well, I'm giving up the rug trade. It's been fine for the summer and I've met lots of folk, but let's face it, there's no real money in it."

Hmm, five grand in six weeks isn't bad, but of course you haven't a clue how to *buy* the damn things. I could show you if you like."

"Thanks, Harry, but no, I've been looking into something else," I said, my imagination now ablaze. "I met a chap in La Mamola who wants me to do some driving for him."

"What? In Bambi?"

"Yes… or rather no. I could use Bambi, but he's got a fleet of vans, so I'll use one of those. I'll be mainly travelling up and down the east coast."

"Shifting what?"

"Oh, mostly foodstuff. It's a steady job and I'll be legal, so I might settle down somewhere, as I don't fancy spending the winter in Bambi."

"And is there real money in *that*? I wouldn't have thought so."

"Oh, it's pretty well paid, but no doubt I'll start a sideline of some sort at some point."

"Ha, don't go getting yourself involved in smuggling, eh?"

"Ha ha, not likely."

"Right, that's enough chatter. They arrive a week from today, so we'll expect you soon after. Jeremy says he's looking forward to catching up."

"He might have called me."

"Ah, no, his phone broke and he's got a new one, so he lost your number, though his is still the same."

"That explains it. I'd have called you, and him, but I can't put any more credit on my phone here."

"We've survived. Bye then."

"Bye, Harry."

I ordered a beer from the waiter and quickly reviewed my performance, giving myself nine out of ten, plus a pat on the back for saving myself a face-to-face inquisition, always trickier where Harry was involved. Yes, now it would be pleasant to see both my pals, plus spouses, with a clear conscience and a viable plan for the winter. I drank my beer, had a swim and ordered a glass of wine, so when the phone rang again I was feeling pretty perky about my impending rendezvous with you know who.

11

"Hola," I purred into the phone.

"Geoff, it's me, Claudia."

"Hi, baby."

"No problems?"

"No, all fine. When do I see you?"

"Well, I'm in Madrid right now. You'll be pleased to hear that I have another job for you."

"Yes, I look forward to hearing about it."

"I'm going to tell you now. I'm on a payphone."

"No, honey, I want to hear it from your own lips."

"These are my own lips, Geoff."

I cuffed myself. "I didn't mean that. I meant that I want to see you."

"You will, I promise, after your next job."

"Nah."

"What?"

"Nah, meaning no. I insist on seeing you, as I have some slight... well, we need to speak face to face."

"But I'm in Madrid."

"That's OK. You head south until you see the sea, then go left a bit, or right a bit, till you reach Torre del Mar, or Torrox Costa, as that's where I am now, chilling out at a swell hotel," I said with great nonchalance, for I didn't mean to take no for an answer.

"After the job. Listen, on Sunday the 25th at—"

"Whoa, sweetie! Don't waste your breath. Geoff Corless won't be moving an inch till he's seen you."

"A what?"

"An inch. About two and a half centimetres. I can never remember if it's 2.45 or 2.54 centimetres, but what the hell, I'm not budging till I've seen you, comprendes?"

"Look, Geoff, I'm your superior and you'll do what you're damn well told. Are you going to listen to the instructions, or not?"

I sipped my wine, then whistled tunefully for a while, before asking the hovering waiter for another glass, it being the second time I'd inadvertently called him.

"So, when do I see you?" I finally asked.

"You don't. If you're not careful you'll be out of a job, Geoff."

"OK, babe. I'll tell you what I'm going to do now."

"What?"

"I'm going to go to my room – a large one, overlooking the sea – and get dressed. Then I'm going to get into Bambi and go for a drive."

"What are you getting at, for God's sake?"

"I'm going to drive to Torre del Mar."

"But I'm not there."

"I'm going to drive to Torre del Mar and then turn off down a little lane. I shall drive down that lane until I reach a certain house, whereupon I shall ring the bell, or scale the fence, and speak to my *real* boss, a Belgian man called... Hu-go," I said, feeling that I'd got the dramatic effect just right.

"He... he's not there either."

"He-he's? What's that supposed to mean?" I said, taking my inspiration from the grand inquisitor Harry.

"He's not there."

"Then I shall camp outside the gate until he returns. In a van like Bambi if one uses the water frugally one can camp autonomously for up to a fortnight. What do you say to that, you little lynx?"

She sighed, a sigh of capitulation, I knew, for I'd often heard them before. "Oh, all right then. I'll come and see you this evening."

"Fast driver, are you?"

"Yes, very. What's the name of your hotel?"

"The Iberostar. You can't miss it."

"I know it."

"Go to reception and have them escort you to my room."

"No, Geoff, we'll meet on the restaurant terrace at about nine."

"All right, we'll have some dinner first then. I shall await you with open arms."

"Hmm, I hope you've got a good reason for dragging me back from Madrid."

"Several. Until nine, my precious," I said, and hung up without another word.

During my numerous shopping trips with that vixen Alina I had also taken the opportunity to buy a few casual rags for myself, so when Claudia arrived at ten past nine I greeted her wearing my beige Abercrombie & Fitch jacket, my lemony-hued Van Heusen shirt and my green Versace jeans, not to mention my modest Next brogues, bought on a day when Alina gave my wallet an especially hard hammering. Claudia was dressed demurely in a white blouse, blue slacks and low-heeled shoes, but she looked ravishing all the same. A Jeeves-like waiter escorted us to our secluded table, whereupon I slipped him a tenner, ordered a bottle of champagne to get the old gastric juices flowing, and eyed Claudia enigmatically across the table, for I meant to maintain my psychological advantage throughout the meal and on into the wee hours.

"So, Claudia, here we are at last," I said suavely.

"Yes, Geoff, here we are, at great inconvenience to myself," she said sulkily, though I could see she was impressed by our surroundings, not that she'd be short of a bob or two herself, as she probably made as much money as me, but still, she was seeing me in my natural environment for the first time and behind her stony stare I could detect a certain yearning, but I had to clear up the Lo Campano conundrum before moving onto more agreeable matters.

When the waiter returned with the bubbly, Claudia claimed to have little appetite, so I ordered for both of us, and as they didn't have oysters I insisted that the salad contain an abundance of celery, asparagus and avocado, due to the aphrodisiacal qualities I'd discovered that same afternoon on my phone.

I topped up her glass and cleared my throat. "Now, Claudia dear, there's something that's been... not exactly bothering me, but perturbing me slightly."

"It's the same thing, isn't it?"

"Let's just say that it's been flitting around in this little head of mine and that I won't feel completely comfortable until you explain the reason for it," I said, before raising my palms, lowering them, raising my glass, clinking hers and smiling.

"I can't, Geoff."

"Why not, honeybun?"

"Because I don't know what it is."

"Ah, well... well, can you guess?" I asked, having always been fond of the occasional guessing game, something that Jeremy lampooned mercilessly in his scrappy little book, to very little humorous effect.

She scanned the adjacent tables, all empty. "Did you expect more money for the last job?" she murmured.

"No, I considered my remuneration adequate."

"Did you not like the arrangements in La Isleta?"

"They were fine," I said, resisting the temptation to tell her that she was getting warm.

"The route?"

"Spot on."

"You don't like working at night?"

"No, I'm on the ball 24/7."

"What?"

"I'm on the ball day and night."

"What?"

"I'm prepared for every eventuality, around the clock."

"Oh, right. Well in that case I can't imagine what it is that's bothering you."

"I'll give you a clue; two words."

"More money?"

"No, I've told you I was happy with my pay."

"I mean next time."

"Oh, well, a bit more wouldn't go amiss. Now, those two words. They're the name of a place."

Her bonny brow ruffled. "Carta… no, Cartagena's one word. I give up, Geoff."

"The first word is Lo."

She scratched her head and smoothed her glossy hair. "Lo… Lo… Lo Campano, you mean?"

"Yes, Lo Campano. How can you explain that choice of destination?"

"But isn't it obvious, Geoff?" she said with a becoming titter.

I tittered back. "Not to me, it isn't."

"But don't you see? It's the last place anyone would expect us to make a delivery of valuable truffles. The food police have had every Michelin star restaurant in Spain under surveillance since the white truffle season began. Lo Campano's right off their radar. It was Hugo's idea and it's brilliant."

"Yes... no, wait. Who on earth are the food police?"

"La *Policía Alimenticia*? Haven't you heard of them? Well, few people have, as they're pretty secret. They're a small but elite branch of the *Policía Nacional* and they've cut a swathe through the food smuggling trade during the last couple of years," she said, or words to that effect.

I grunted, sipped and sighed. "I'm not sure I believe you, Claudia. Lo Campano is a drug-dealing mecca and it's a little fishy you having me deliver sealed boxed there in the dead of night."

She gasped and put her hand to her prettily gaping mouth. "Ugh, don't mention that word! I've told you that Hugo is dead against drugs. Why... his own son died of an overdose just a few years ago, so the very idea... I mean, Geoff, please," she wailed, quietly, before grasping my hand.

I allowed her to knead it for a while as I gazed at the sparkling pool, my lips pursed and my eyes narrowed.

"Hmm," I said, and nothing more.

"Well, I hope that's cleared up your silly little doubt, Geoff," she said, stroking my fingers.

"Yes, it has..." Her hand slipped away. "*But...*" She grasped it again. "What if the *normal* police want to search my van, eh?"

"Ha, ha, then the joke will be on them, won't it?"

"Will it?"

"Of course. The normal police can't do a *thing* about truffles. They probably won't even know what they are."

I moved my head from side to side, before laying my left hand on the table, which she grasped, so I freed my right in order to take a drink and avoid either of us getting our sleeves in the salad.

"They might ask me what I'm doing in a camper van behind a petrol station near one of the worst *barrios* in Spain in the middle of the night, mightn't they?"

"I've told you before what you have to do if the police ever stop you."

"Yes."

"Do you remember?"

"Yes."

"What is it?"

"Er, just act cool."

"Yes, but above all remember that you're a silly *guiri* on holiday in a ludicrous van."

"Yes, I guess I could pretend to be one of those."

"You tell them you were tired and just pulled over at the nearest petrol station to get some sleep, in English of course."

"Of course. Here comes the fish dish."

As we scoffed the salmon – an aphrodisiac of some renown – I mulled over our recent exchange and had to admit that Claudia's logic, though convoluted, made perfect sense. In the world of smuggling one has to think outside the box, so I chuckled to think that while the dastardly Axel – whose truffle trade Hugo was in the process of pinching – was sending his vans straight into the arms of the food police, we were blazing a cunning trail via a cesspit that no-one would suspect, though one minor point remained unexplained.

"Er, Claudia, how do the truffles get from Lo Campano to the restaurants, if not in vans?"

She chewed away slowly until her mouth was completely empty, nodding all the while. "I shouldn't tell you that, Geoff, as ours is a compartmentalised organisation, but if you promise not to breathe a word I don't mind letting you know, in general terms."

"Fire away, as even under torture I wouldn't reveal a thing."

"Well, it's simple really. Cars, motorcycles and bicycles."

"Really? All three?"

"Yes, and in that order. In the case of your first job, each of the three boxes was taken by car to destinations F, G and H, where the boxes were split and motorcycles carried them onwards to points P, Q, R and so on – six in all – where the truffles were further divided and ridden by bicycle to… well, to the restaurants. Is that clear?"

"As crystal. It's brilliant, foolproof," I said, certain that a woman, no matter how intelligent, could make up something like that.

My mind finally at rest, I ordered a red wine to accompany the veal, which arrived presently.

"Ugh, this is absolutely covered in garlic, Geoff."

"Yes, garlic is a great… garnish. What's my next job then?" I asked, keen to knock the shop talk on the head and get down to the serious business of the evening.

"It's ever so simple. On Sunday the 25th at 0100 hours you drive to exactly the same place as last time. In fact, your instructions are identical in every respect. Do you still remember them?"

By way of reply I smiled and tapped my temple, before wiping the grease from my hair, having forgotten to put down my fork.

"Good. Same times, same places. The only difference is that the load will be bigger and your envelope thicker."

"Suits me, sugar."

"Now please ask the waiter to take this revolting mess away. I've eaten enough anyway and I must be off soon."

"Come, come, Claudia. The night is young and so are we."

She sighed and took my hand once again. "Geoff, thanks to you I've just driven five hundred kilometres and will have to drive five hundred more early tomorrow morning."

I opened my mouth, but she placed a finger on my lips, before caressing my chin.

"Geoff, in Madrid I'm in the process of expanding our truffle business to the rest of Europe and it's vital that I'm back there by midday tomorrow."

"Is Hugo there too?"

She cleared her throaty daintily. "Hugo's in Florence, talking to potential suppliers. He'll be there for as long as it takes."

"To wrest the whole show away from Axel, eh?"

She gulped gracefully on hearing that awful name. "That's right. These are crucial times for our enterprise, Geoff, and it's important that we all play our parts well."

"Of course. So, no time for coffee then?"

"I'm afraid not."

"My room's just over there, beyond the pool."

"Yes, you must be tired too."

"Oh, Claudia!" I declaimed, pushing my chair back and rising to my full height. "Come with me now and we'll make the earth move! By midnight we'll both be sated and you can get some shuteye."

Claudia had remained seated, but then smiled in such an alluring, almost hypnotic way that I flopped back down into my chair.

"Oh, Geoff, Geoff, what am I going to do with you?"

"Anything you like."

She stood up and floated around the table, before standing by my side and grasping the nape of my neck, which she began to stroke in a most soothing way.

"Listen, I'm going to make you a promise that I promise I won't break," she whispered in my left ear.

"Hmm, a double promise, eh? Let's hear it."

"When you return from your next mission I will come and spend the *whole* week here with you," she murmured, before nibbling my ear lobe, kneading my neck and stroking my thigh with her free hand – the left, it must have been – so you can imagine that the threefold sensory impact was significant, but despite the instant rush of blood to my loins I remained clearheaded enough to suspect that this was yet another attempt to fob me off.

"That sounds marvellous, sweetheart, but how can I be *sure*?"

"Because I promised," she crooned, still kneading, stroking and, best of all, nibbling.

Then I had one of my brainwaves. "Listen, honey, unless I'm absolutely sure that you'll be mine after my mission, I'm not sure I can carry it off."

"Of *course* you can, my brave soldier of fortune." (Knead, stroke, nibble.) "How can you doubt me when you see how you arouse me?"

"I'm not touching you. I can't, I'm all tied up," I said, fearing that my Versaces were about to burst open, despite the unquestionable quality of the stitching.

She ceased to nibble and sighed instead, before looking at her watch, which gave me yet another idea.

"Ha, leave me your watch as a keepsake, dear."

"But it's a Baume & Mercier."

"They won't mind."

"I mean, it cost me over €3000."

"It'll be safe with me," I said, taking a liking to its silvery face and quaint little stones. "You can take mine if you like, then we'll both have something to remind us of each other."

She fingered my wrist, having by then ceased to paw me. "But it's a pile of... it's a cheap one."

"Yes, I was going to buy a good one, but I ran… into cash flow problems."

"Oh, very well. Take it, but look after it. My… father bought it for me."

I deftly removed her timepiece and slipped it into my shirt pocket, before unclipping my Casio. "Here you are, darling. Maybe when you look into its face you'll see me."

"Maybe." She popped my watch into her little bag, stooped to kiss me on the lips, and made to rise, but I clutched her arm and pulled her close.

"Claudia, let me taste your tongue before you go," I pleaded.

"It'll just taste of garlic," she said, pulling a face, because of the garlic.

"Nevertheless."

She then closed her eyes – so shy, so shy – and gave me a brief but thorough snog which took my breath away, so much so that when I came to my senses she had flown.

"Ah, Claudia," I murmured to her receding figure.

"Can I get you anything else, señor?" said the waiter, having shimmered silently over during the latter part of our entanglement.

"Isn't she lovely?"

"Yes sir, a familiar face."

"You mean she's been here before, with… other men?" I growled, suddenly consumed by jealously.

He raised his eyebrows a fraction of an inch. "I refer, sir, to her particular type of beauty, more often seen on the cinema screen. Anything else, sir?"

"Coffee and cognac, my man, and thank you for your kind attentions."

"It's been a pleasure, sir."

12

Although the Iberostar Hotel wasn't cheap I stayed there until the eve of my mission, when I checked out, loaded Bambi and headed off towards Cabo de Gata, reaching the beach parking area at La Isleta del Moro at 0058 hours. I parked some distance from two empty cars and strolled into the village, but instead of heading for the jetty I hung around near a restaurant terrace from where I could see the landing beach. At 0121 hours I heard the purring of a craft and could make out its outline under the starry sky, but just then a door slammed shut and I saw a man locking up the restaurant. Having by then taken a seat on one of the handy plastic chairs, I remembered my instructions and allowed my head to slump forward and my legs splay out in what I hoped would resemble a drunken daze, and when footsteps approached I hiccoughed loudly for good measure.

I felt a tap on the shoulder.

"Time for home, amigo," said a deep, kindly voice.

I groaned and muttered, before raising my head to see a fat, white-shirted chap peering down at me.

I grunted. "Drank too much," I mumbled.

"I can see that. Never mind, get yourself off to bed now. Where are you staying?"

"Bambi beach," I muttered, as when I play a part it suffuses my whole being, so I really did feel as drunk as a lord and far less cunning than usual.

"What's that? Apartments? I haven't heard of them."

"No, Bambi camper van, near beach."

"Oh, I see. Well, I'll drive you there."

That sobered me up somewhat. "No, no, I'll walk. Need the air," I said, pushing myself to my feet.

"OK, but don't drive anywhere."

"Course not. Thanks anyway."

The man then cupped his ear with his hand and frowned. "Hmm, sounds like the smugglers are here again."

"The what?"

"The smugglers. That beach is a popular spot for them. Speedboats, dinghies, you name it; they arrive most weeks in summer. We just turn a blind eye, but they must be bloody stupid if they think we don't know. Look, you'd better stay here for a while longer. You don't want to bump into those bastards."

"No, I'll sit awhile and take the air."

"You sound a bit better already. When you hear the boat go, wait for half an hour and then it'll be safe, as they don't hang around."

"Will do."

"Ha, in my father's day when they just brought tobacco he'd sometimes wander over and buy a few boxes, but since they started smuggling people and drugs we stay well out of the way. It's an awful business nowadays, but they're dangerous people and we're scared to report them in case of reprisals."

"Shocking folk. Exploiters. Need locking up," I drawled, wishing he would go.

"Yes. You know, I've a good mind to call the cops right now. It's about time someone made a stand and helped to catch the devils."

"Throw away the key," I mumbled. "Too late now though. Gone soon. Better call cops next time."

"Hmm, maybe you're right. I'll be off then," he said, patting my shoulder.

"Buenas noches," I said, before watching him saunter up the street.

A close call, I thought, but I'd handled him well. Resolving to tell Claudia that a change of rendezvous might be advisable in future, I bided my time until 0220 and strolled back to Bambi, my keen, carrot-fuelled eyes perceiving that she'd sunk a few inches, denoting a bumper crop of truffles. Sure enough, on shining my torch I saw a total of eight boxes in the back, so, anticipating a five-figure payday, or paynight, I started her up, eased her onto the road and roared away towards the motorway. My encounter with the agreeable restaurant owner might have shaken a lesser man, but as I ploughed my lonely furrow along the narrow road I felt sure that he would now be sound asleep after a hard day's work, which made my mind turn to my own future. As that close call had illustrated, smuggling wasn't the securest of occupations, and during my week between the sheets with Claudia I might try to convince her to forsake her easy but essentially dishonest life and join me in some sort of legitimate enterprise.

Failing that I would hand in my notice and invest my earnings in something kosher, a plan which would make my forthcoming meeting with Harry, Jeremy *et al* more relaxed, as Harry would undoubtedly quiz me regarding my supposed driving job, forcing me to be on my guard day and night, as he was quite capable of shaking me awake in the early hours to clear up some technical point. Yes, I decided as I drove past the town of Vera, this would be my last ever smuggling run, no matter how persuasive Claudia's pillow talk proved to be, and from now on I'd toe the line and put my nose to the grindstone, though I'd miss the money, that's for sure.

Timing my arrival to perfection, I parked up behind the Repsol garage at 0529 hours, placed the key under the mat, softy closed the door and walked into the arms of two masked men. The two hefty chaps wordlessly linked their arms with mine and marched me back to Bambi, by which time two cars had arrived which were simply stuffed with masked men, who all jumped out and rushed away into the shadows, before the cars departed as quickly as they had come.

"You're a bit early," I said. "Unless the time on my mobile is wrong. I left my watch with a friend, you see, so I've had to rely on my phone. It is half five, isn't it?"

"Get in the back," said the taller of the two impassive chaps.

"I'll have to get the key from under the mat, but aren't I supposed to clear off now?"

"Open the back door," said the shorter of the two, a mere six footer.

I complied and soon found myself seated on a box of truffles, while my companions lifted a few more onto the right-hand bed, sat down on the left-hand bed, checked that the curtains were fully closed and unsheathed their handguns.

"A bit over the top, what?" I said, not feeling altogether comfortable with these unexpected developments.

"Be quiet," said the tall one.

We sat silently for a while and whenever I opened my mouth to speak I saw the gunmetal glint of the tall one's weapon, pointed at me, so I resigned myself to waiting, while cursing Claudia for not having apprised me of this curious change of plan, but it wasn't long before all hell broke loose, as no sooner had a vehicle pulled up alongside than I heard a lot of shouting, followed by several shots plus a quick burst from an automatic weapon, after which there were sundry shuffling, grunting and clicking sounds, followed by the screech of multiple tyres, more grunting and shuffling, the slamming of doors and more tyre screeching. The silence which followed was rather eerie, until the crackle of a radio enabled me to begin to grasp what was going on.

The shorter man switched on a torch and spoke into his receiver, saying that the suspect had been apprehended, to which his interlocutor responded by telling him to register the vehicle before bringing him, meaning me, in. So they were cops, I finally twigged, and when a mischievous grin appeared on my face the tall one asked me what the hell I was smiling at.

"Oh, nothing, but I think you'll find that there's been some kind of mistake," I said, as at this stage I saw little point in pretending to be a daft English tourist, having said several things in Spanish when I'd still thought they were just overzealous colleagues.

"Let's get the prick to drive this thing to the station," said the tall one, which I thought rather unprofessional, to say the least.

"I'm only carrying food… for a friend," I said.

"Food, you call it? You sick bastard," said the shorter one, before removing his mask to reveal a young, stern, stubbly face.

"They're just truffles; not the chocolate ones, but the ones that pigs sniff out, though they prefer to use–"

"Shut your f*cking mouth, you foreign scum," said the tall one, his now maskless face reminding me of Harry's in his younger days; smooth, fleshy and thuggish, though it has mellowed a bit over the years.

"Let's open a box and see, Paco," said the shorter one.

"We're not supposed to open them yet."

"Let's just check out this little runt's story before we take him in," said Paco, producing a penknife from his pocket.

"You're going to feel pretty damn silly in a minute, you lanky streak of piss," I said, not taking kindly to being called a runt, let alone a little one.

"What did he just say?" Paco asked the shorter and as yet nameless one.

"God knows. Where are you from? Albania?"

"I'm from the *British* Isles, you lanky *idiot*," I hissed, which earned me a clip round the earhole.

"That's assault, you beast! Just wait till the British embassy hears about this. The ambassador is my... uncle, I'll have you know."

"Must be bloody old then."

"Ha, go on, open a box and prepare to eat your words!" I thundered.

Paco slit open a box and shone his torch inside. "What do these truffles look like then?" he asked me in a low voice.

"Ha, I *told* you so. Now, as you're not the food police you'd better let me go pretty damn quick, and those poor men they've just whisked away too," I said. I was about to also mention my lost wages, but thought better of it, fortunately as it turned out.

"What the f*ck is this cretin on about, Manolo?"

"Search me."

"So, what do these truffles look like?" Paco asked again, the flap of the box still obscuring my view.

As I'd never clapped eyes on a truffle in my life, apart from chocolate ones, I wasn't sure how to respond, but as I knew that my liberty might depend on it I tried to buy some time.

"Well, they look sort of truffly, don't they?"

Paco's head fell and he shook it. "You'll have to do better than that."

"Well, look, you know chocolate truffles?" I asked them both.

"I think so," said Manolo.

"I've eaten the odd one at Christmas," said Paco.

"Well, they're the same shape and… sort of texture as real truffles."

He tapped the box. "What colour are these truffles?"

"Why, white, of course," I said with a beatific smile.

"So is this."

"What?"

"This powder." He lifted a plastic bag, made a small incision with his penknife, dipped in his finger and licked it. "Cocaine. Pure stuff too. You're f*cked, pal."

"There's been a terrible mistake."

***

Back at the police station I sat in my clean but spartan cell and mulled over recent events. Someone had deceived me, I knew that, but had it been Claudia or Hugo himself? There was no doubt in my mind that I was in a spot of bother, but I meant to stick to my truffle story and hope that my previously unblemished record would convince them that I wouldn't have touched cocaine with a bargepole had I known I was transporting it. As they seemed to be in no hurry to question me I had plenty of time to ponder over how best to defend myself, and I concluded that I ought to say that a nameless beauty had seduced me in Torrox Costa, before asking me to transport the load of truffles as a special favour to her. Being a sucker for skirt, I would tell them, I had agreed to this seemingly innocent proposal and thus landed myself in my present predicament, after which I would put my trust in the Spanish legal system and hopefully get off with a slap on the wrist and maybe a fine.

Several hours after my arrest – for there was no other word for it – I was led first to a bathroom to freshen up and then into a small office where two casually dressed fellows awaited me. The older one – a thin, balding, hatchet-faced man in his fifties – perused me with polite interest while the younger one – a cheerful, fresh-faced lad in his late twenties – offered me coffee.

"That's very kind of you."

"Milk and sugar?"

"Yes, please," I said, as though I don't normally take sugar – already being sweet enough, as the saying goes – I thought it advisable to keep my blood sugar levels up during the course of the questioning, not having eaten for about fourteen hours and having had only the briefest of snoozes in my cell.

While the youngster was away the older man continued to eye me, but when I began to speak he bade me wait for his colleague, as they intended to record our conversation.

"For posterity, eh?"

"Yes."

The young chap returned with three plastic cups, handed me mine and switched on a digital recorder on the large table between us. In a very businesslike voice the older man announced to the microphone that the questioning of Cheffrey Charles Corless was about to begin at 11.15am on Sunday the 25th of September. He then looked at his colleague, who began to speak.

"Now, Cheffrey, can you–"

"Just Geoff, please. No-one calls me Geoffrey."

"Chef?"

"Geoff."

"Chef."

I chuckled. "That'll do. Everyone called me Chef in Jaén when I used to live there."

To my surprise they exchanged a meaningful look on hearing this and the older man made a quick note, which I leant over to see, but the spoilsport covered it with his hand.

"OK… Chef," the younger man went on. "I want you to tell us exactly what–"

"Uh-oh, I think you've given me the wrong coffee," I said. "No sugar in this one."

"Sorry, I forgot," he said, before producing a sachet of sugar and a plastic stick from his jacket pocket and handing them over.

"Thanks, I don't usually take sugar, but I just fancied it. Sorry, what were you saying…er?"

"Jorge," said the younger man. "I'm Jorge and this is Isidro. We're about to question you regarding a very serious offence, so please think carefully about what you say."

"Oh, I have already, though it's really quite simple and I think you'll find that you're making a mountain out of a molehill."

"Out of a what?" asked Isidro, his pen poised.

"A molehill. One of those hills, or rather mounds, that a mole makes, normally on lawns, or at least that's where they're most noticeable, though I guess they make them all over the place, regardless of what lies above them."

"Tell us what happened," he said sharply. "You're only making it worse for yourself by talking such nonsense."

Jorge patted his older colleague on the arm, upon which he leant his head back and exhaled noisily, before attempting to look at me in a kindly way, though I could see he was miffed, probably about having to work on a Sunday.

"Chef, in your own time, tell us what happened," said Jorge.

"Well, it all began about a week ago in the town of Torrox Costa," I began, and proceeded to spin them a yarn about having met a woman very much like Claudia at the Hotel Iberostar. I had wined her and dined her with the proceeds of my summer rug sales, but the little minx wouldn't agree to consummate our relationship until I'd done a little favour for her. Her van had broken down, she said, so could I possibly transport some truffles from La Isleta del Moro to Cartagena for her? I saw no harm in this, so I drove there and at the appointed time left Bambi, my camper van, to be loaded by her pals, after which I had driven to Lo Campano.

"There your colleagues met me, there was quite a kerfuffle, and here we are," I said, smiling, raising my hands and letting them fall into my lap with a conclusive slap.

"Yes, here we are," Isidro muttered, confirming my suspicion that he'd been done out of a Sunday.

"What was the name of the young woman?" Jorge asked me.

"Carlota," I said off the top of my head. "That's what she called herself anyway," I added craftily.

"What did she look like?"

I proceeded to describe Claudia down to the last detail. I'd initially intended to describe Alina or a combination of Claudia and Alina, but fearing that I might get mixed up I settled on Claudia in the end, as there are tons of tanned, slim, dark-haired, brown-eyed women in Spain, though none quite as divinely beautiful as her.

"She sounds very attractive," said Jorge.

"Oh, yes," I said dreamily.

"So it's unsurprising that you fell in with her criminal plans."

"Yes, or rather no. Fall in with her plans, yes, but in good faith, plus a burning desire to get into her knickers. She didn't look like a criminal at all. She told me that she once considered becoming a nun," I said, just to add colour to my account, which appeared to be going down like a house on fire. "I will admit to one thing though," I added.

"What?" they asked in unison.

"Well, it now seems pretty clear to me that Clau… Carlota was trying to avoid paying tax by transporting the truffles in that way. As I've become implicated, though against my will, I suppose I ought to make good those payments out of my rug money."

They exchanged a baffled glance and Isidro, after clenching his rather yellow teeth, was about to speak, but Jorge patted his arm again.

"Chef, there weren't any truffles. Can you not grasp that?"

"Ha, sorry, Jorge! I'd forgotten about that nasty stuff in the boxes," I said, which was true, as I'd had truffles on the brain all summer long.

They then exchanged another perplexed glance, before Jorge stopped the recorder and suggested to Isidro that they might be as well to consult Doctor Casillas.

"I think he's bullshitting, but as you wish," said old misery guts.

"Who's Doctor Casillas?" I asked.

"The psychiatric consultant."

"A loony doctor, eh? I think he'll find that I'm as sane as a… as the next man."

"Who's the next man?" Isidro asked abruptly. "An associate?"

"No, it's an expression, in English anyway."

"We can do nothing more here for now," said Jorge, beginning to rise.

"I'm going home then," said Isidro.

"I *knew* you'd been called in at the last minute because of this silly misunderstanding, Isidro. I'm really sorry," I said, rising to my feet. "Can I give you a lift home?" I added; a vain hope, I knew, but I rather liked the impression I'd made so far – of a gullible but innocent man – and planned to keep it up.

"You'll be taken back to the cell, I'm afraid," said Jorge, but just then we heard a knock on the door and Isidro was summoned outside.

When he returned a few minutes later with a sheet of paper in his hand his rosy countenance suggested that he had cast off his Sunday blues. Smiling like a shark, he handed the sheet to Jorge and proceeded to cackle like an especially vindictive witch.

"Sod my nephew's baptism party, this is going to be *much* more fun," he said, his beady eyes boring into mine in a most malevolent way.

Jorge, on the other hand, after perusing both sides of the sheet, became deathly pale. After casting me a rather aggrieved glance he shuffled over to the photocopier and made three copies, before handing the original to a copper outside, closing the door, handing copies to Isidro and me, and slumping into his chair.

"I'll take over now," said Isidro, rubbing his bony hands together before switching on the recorder. "How do you explain this document, Chef?"

Having been intrigued by the metamorphosis of my senior questioner I hadn't looked at the sheet, but when I did I saw it was a copy of my street plan of the Peñamefécit area of Jaén. Nothing to get excited about, I thought, as I'd already mentioned that I'd spent the summer selling rugs.

"Ah, yes, I went to Jaén to sell rugs, and also to visit my old haunts, as I lived there many years ago," I said, allowing the sheet to float onto the table.

"We'll come back to the map. Now turn it over," said Isidro, grinning like a demented cheetah.

On the other side I saw the notes I'd scribbled after Claudia had thrown a wobbly and pointed her gun at me. For the benefit of those of you who don't have photographic memories I shall reproduce them here:

Claudia would never have pulled the trigger.
Carmela's brothers will never spot me.
The guns are (probably) for those valiant boys in blue.
I'm going to get paid tons of money.

"Ah," I said, pursing my lips and nodding slowly.

"Now, Chef, would you be so kind as to go through these notes point by point and explain their significance to us?" said Isidro, his hands clasped as if in prayer.

"Yes, of course. Do you both understand these English phrases?"

"Oh, yes."

"Can I choose where to start?"

"Be my guest."

"Well, this one about Carmela's brothers is pretty clear."

"Not to us, it isn't."

"Well, over twenty years ago I went to work at a language school in Jaén," I began, and boy did I give them a story to remember, or forget, as I purposefully made it as pedantic and boring as I could. After telling them about Carmela and her family in mind-numbing detail it was easy to explain the phrase about the brothers never spotting me, and by glancing surreptitiously at my crib sheet from time to time I was able to clear up each of the other three points to my satisfaction and their despair:

A pretty girl called Claudia had been a jealous rival for my affections and once, while drunk at the local fiestas, had threatened Carmela with a fairground gun.

Carmela's brothers – Pablo, Paco and Pepe – had stockpiled so many hunting weapons between them that it seemed inevitable that the police would eventually confiscate them and add them to their own arsenal.

Having been recently unemployed back in Britain, my generous wages seemed like a fortune compared to my dole money.

It was at this point, when I began to describe the trials and tribulations of my pre-Jaén days, that Isidro switched off the recorder and emitted a heartrending moan, before laying his head on the table and beginning to bang it rhythmically, until Jorge placed his hand between his skull and the wood and uttered a few soothing words. Isidro then lifted his head, wiped his red, bleary eyes, and turned to his colleague.

"I can't believe I'm hearing this, Jorge," he whimpered. "In thirty years on the force I've never come across anything like this before. I think I'm going mad."

"You're just overworked, Isidro. Can't you see that it's him who's deranged?"

"I am most certainly *not* deranged, young man," I protested, but I aimed a loopy sort of look in his direction, as it occurred to me that it would be no bad thing if they began to doubt my sanity. "You asked me to explain my nostalgic note and I did so to the best of my ability."

Jorge looked at the recorder. "Chef, you've been talking for almost two hours and we're none the wiser."

"You asked me to explain my nostalgic note and I did so to the best of my ability," I repeated, as mad folk are apt to do that. "Why you are so interested in what I did twenty years ago, I don't know, but… I say."

"What?"

"That spider on the window has just moved for the first time since we've been here."

"Probably sick to death of the shite you've been talking," Isidro muttered. "They'll be sitting down to lunch now and I've paid for that with the bloody present we bought."

Jorge patted his clenched hand. "I'll take over now, Isidro, and we'll wind things up as soon as we can."

Thus it was that the following ticklish matter was skirted over rather more briefly than it might have been.

"Chef, let's go back to the map," said Jorge after switching on the recorder yet again.

I turned mine over. "Ah, Peñamefécit, where Carmela used to live," I enthused. "Did I tell you how I used to throw pebbles up at the window before serenading her on my banjo?"

"Yes, you told us that. Now, Chef, it just happens that a few days ago an Islamic terrorist cell was discovered in that part of Jaén. A large arsenal of weapons was seized and several foreign nationals detained. You wouldn't happen to know anything about that, would you?"

"Not a thing, Jorge. I drove past Carmela's old flat, then tried to hawk a few rugs in the city centre. After that I spent a while chatting to an old acquaintance in a bar, before heading back into the country, as I always sold more rugs in the villages. The thing about rugs is that–"

Jorge raised a clammy hand. "Not now, Chef. We may wish to interview your acquaintance in the bar."

"Be my guest. She's a large lady called Marta," I said, before happily giving him the name of the establishment, as Marta's distorted memories would only serve to confirm my suspected loopiness.

Jorge switched off the recorder and asked Isidro if he thought they ought to follow that line of enquiry.

"God, no, they'll send us there on a wild goose chase and we'll never see the back of this freak."

"But the terrorist cell, in the very same place?"

"Does he look like the sort of person who'd deal with terrorists?"

"Well, they're a bit mad too."

"Not like him."

"They're evil bombers, while I'm just a gigolo," I said, before launching into the song.

"Shut up!" Isidro shrieked, finally getting some colour back into those chiselled cheeks.

"One final question, Chef," said Jorge after stroking Isidro's arm. "How did you come by the money we found in the van? Almost four thousand euros."

"Rugs. I've done with rugs now though and I'm going to move into… fishing tackle."

"Why's that?" asked Isidro through his folded arms, having just slumped over the table.

"Oh, I don't know… I like the floats, flies and other lures. They're so colourful, aren't they?" I said, looking dreamily at Jorge.

"Doctor Casillas, tomorrow, first thing," Isidro muttered.

"All right, Chef, that's the end of our first interview," said Jorge, also looking a little the worse for wear.

"You mean we'll be having more?" I asked with enthusiasm, though I refrained from clapping, not wishing to overdo things.

Then came a second knock on the door, but as Isidro was in no state to respond, Jorge trudged over and stepped outside.

"You'll still have time to go to that baptism party," I said to the top of Isidro's head.

"Go to hell," came his muffled reply.

"Sorry I spoke."

Jorge returned, the fresh sparkle in his eyes evaporating on seeing my encouraging smile.

"What's new, Jorge?"

"Claudia has been arrested."

Isidro lifted his head and rubbed his eyes.

"What, after all these years?" I said. "No, you don't understand. Those fairground guns were fastened to the counter. Even if she'd wanted to shoot Carmela she couldn't have aimed at her properly, unless Carmela had stepped into the stall, which–"

"No, no, not *that* Claudia. We suspect that the Claudia in question might be the young woman who tricked you into delivering the coke."

"But that was Carlota."

"She uses several aliases. She's been under surveillance for some time and was arrested while boarding a plane for Brazil."

"Well I never."

"What?"

"I'm shocked," I said, and I was, as that put paid to the week of passion she'd promised me, although considering the circumstances of her arrest I doubted she'd have kept her promise, the lousy lynx.

"You look thoughtful, Chef."

"Oh, just thinking about what might have been," I said, though to tell the truth I was simply dying to ask if Hugo had also been detained, but I didn't.

"She's on her way here now and will be interrogated later today."

"Right," I said, stroking my chin to conceal a great big gulp.

"Let's hope that her story corroborates yours, Chef."

"Do you not believe me, Jorge?" I asked with a doe-eyed look.

"By God, we want to," Isidro wailed.

"That's very kind of you, Isidro, thank you," I said, upon which he covered his eyes, stood up, almost tripped over the chair, and left the room.

"He's stressed out," I said.

"Perhaps he will take early retirement after all," Jorge muttered. "Now, Chef, go back to your cell, have something to eat and just pray that Claudia backs up your story."

An image of the black man staring down at me from the space over Bambi's cab passed before my mind's eye, followed by one of shadowy figures hauling large bags up the moonlit beach at Maro.

"I hope so too, but that kind of floozy is capable of making up all sorts of things to get herself off the hook. Oh, how she deceived me!"

"Well, fingers crossed, Chef. I think we all want to resolve this muddle as soon as possible," he said, a little tick appearing on his cheek that I hadn't seen before.

12+1

Back in the cell I was given a hearty meal and during the rest of the day many people opened the little hatch to have a look at me, so I always waved and gave them a charming smile. In the evening a policeman entered with another meal and asked me when I wished to make my call.

"What call?"

"You're allowed one phone call. People normally call their lawyer."

"I don't have one. I've never needed one."

"You do now. Look, I can get your mobile phone so you can see your numbers and you can ring whoever you want. I advise you to do it as soon as possible," said the grave young fellow.

"Jeremy or Harry," I thought aloud.

"What?"

"Just wondering who to call. Harry's likely to go off on one about me being here, so I might ring Jeremy, as he'll be at Laura's now, with his wife June. Hmm, maybe I should face the music and call Harry, as Jeremy's mobile will be expensive to ring and I don't want to abuse your hospitality. I can always ask him to put me on to Jeremy before he blows his top."

The officer backed away towards the cell door. "Just give me a knock to let me know when you're ready," he said, before slipping out and locking the door.

After scoffing some rather dry pork chops and drinking another appalling instant coffee, I yoo-hooed through the hatch and was soon led by the same young cop to a small room with a telephone. After finding Harry's number on my mobile I was about to dial it when I realised that the cop was still hanging around.

"I'm going to make a private call, if you don't mind," I said.

"I have to stay here, I'm afraid."

"Do you speak English?"

"No, not much."

"That's good, because I want to ask my friend to hide a big stash of heroin that we've got over in Malaga."

His smooth face froze. "Wh-what?"

"Ha, only joking. I was bored to death in the cell and just felt like having a laugh," I said with a giggle, though this was all part of my lunatic act.

"I... I'll have to report what you just said."

"Don't be daft, son. The trouble with you coppers is that you can't take a joke. Look, the chap I'm about to call is an ex-cop and he's going to go ballistic when he hears about the scrape I've got myself into. Come a bit closer and you'll hear him."

I dialled.

"Harry, it's me, Geoff."

"You coming up yet?"

"Er, I can't make it just now."

"Why not?"

"I'm in a bit of a pickle."

"A what?"

"He's a bit deaf," I said to the cop, who was leaning over the little table in anticipation.

"Why are you talking Spanish?" said Harry.

"Well, the thing is, I'm in a police station in Cartagena."

"Oh, Christ. Did you crash Bambi, or what?"

"No, Bambi's fine. She's in the compound as we speak."

"What's up then?"

"Well…" I began, before looking at the cop and gritting my teeth in a comical way. "You're not going to believe this, Harry."

"Try me."

Having decided not to beat about the bush, I beckoned the cop closer. "I've been arrested on suspicion of cocaine trafficking," I said, turning the earpiece slightly towards my companion.

"You f*cking WHAT?!" he bellowed.

The two of us creased up with laughter, but while I managed to stifle my cries, the cop hooted merrily.

"Is this some sort of joke, you little twat? I heard someone laughing."

"Oh, that's just the copper who's keeping an eye on me. No, seriously, I really have been accused of that. It's not true of course, though it is in a way, so I might need a bit of legal help or something."

"You've been working for that bastard Hugo, haven't you?" he boomed.

I raised my eyebrows and did a bit of a Stan Laurel impression to amuse the pleasant lad, as he probably didn't want to be inside the nick on a Sunday evening either.

"Well, not directly, but… well, I suppose I have, so, as I say…" The phone clicked and a constant tone followed. "I think he's hung up," I said to the cop, handing him the phone.

"Sí," he said, and put it down.

"Can I make another call?"

"You're not supposed to, but I don't see why not. He sounded really pissed off. Who are you going to call now?"

"Oh, I think I'd better get serious, don't you?"

"Well, yes, as you might be facing up to fifteen years in jail."

"Give over."

"What?"

"You're joking?"

"No, I'm not. That was funny, but please call someone who might be more helpful."

"I'll call Jeremy. He'll know what to do."

After finding his mobile number I dialled it.

"Jeremy, it's Geoff here."

"Yes," he said in little more than a whisper.

"Has Harry mentioned my little predicament?"

"My ears are still ringing."

"So I guess he has."

"Yes. It isn't a joke, is it, Geoff?"

"Afraid not."

"Tell me briefly what happened," he said in his teacher's voice.

Somewhat sobered by the cop's mention of a prison sentence, I told him the whole truth, apart from omitting everything that had happened before my dinner date with Claudia in Torrox Costa.

"So, let me get this straight. This woman, who you believe is connected with Hugo the Belgian, tracked you down to the hotel, got you all hot and bothered, and then asked you to transport white Italian truffles from the coast to Cartagena, in return for future sexual... acquiescence?"

"That's it in a nutshell, Jeremy. Do you not believe me?"

"It sounds just like you, Geoff, but I can't believe one of Hugo's stooges just appeared after all this time and got you to do that. You must have had some contact in the meantime."

I cleared my throat. "Well, Jeremy, I mean to keep my story simple, while also pretending to be slightly off my rocker, so I don't want to elaborate now, as it might confuse me."

"Hmm, all right. Listen, I'll get June to ply Harry with drinks while I speak to Laura. I'll see if she's willing to drive over with me tomorrow. We'll enlist the services of a local lawyer and come to see you as soon as they'll let us. Do you have any money?"

"I've got about three thousand, from my rug sales," I said, thinking it wise to set aside a bob or two for a rainy day.

"Good, you're probably going to need it all. I'll speak to Laura now and hopefully we'll see you tomorrow or the day after."

"Thanks, Jeremy, you're a real pal."

"Yes, shame that we had a long walk planned tomorrow and a trip to Malaga the following day, but never mind," he said, which was his subtle way of saying that it wasn't wholly convenient for him to drive to Cartagena on a mission of mercy.

"I'm at the *Policía Nacional* station, by the way."

"OK."

"And there's a Roman theatre you can visit, with a museum," I said, hoping to lessen the blow.

"See you soon."

"Thanks, Jeremy." I hung up. "He's a real friend," I said to the cop.

"Good. Come on, let's get you back to the cell."

***

I slept like a log that night on the narrow but orthopaedic mattress, but found the following morning slow going, only having a couple of copies of the *Revista Oficial del Cuerpo Nacional de Policía* – the police magazine – with which to while away the time. The little hatch opened and closed just as often as on the previous day, but after a while I found that I could hardly muster a smile, let alone a mad one, such was the feeling of *ennui* – French boredom, worse than any other – which gradually overcame me. When they finally came for me at about five in the afternoon I was in a rotten mood, so on being shown into a tiny room where a small, sombre man of indeterminate age – somewhere between forty-three and forty-eight – awaited me, I just nodded and slumped down onto the chair provided.

"I'm Benito, your lawyer," the serious, smartly dressed chap said.

"I'm Geoff, Geoff Corless."

"I know that, Geoff."

"Hey, you can pronounce my name," I said, managing a faint smile. "The only other Spaniard I know who could pronounce it was… a chap I met in a bar."

"Yes, I speak good English," he said in good English. "If you wish, we can converse in your language."

"No way, José."

"I'm sorry?"

"No dice… Allardyce," I improvised.

"I beg your pardon?"

"Not a chance…" I racked my brains for a rhyming name, without success. "…mate. Hablaremos español."

"Muy bien. Better, I suppose, as you'll have to speak it at the trial."

"Will there be a trial?"

"Of course."

"With a judge and jury and… all that?"

"Hmm, I think that will be determined by what is occurring in another room right now. The woman Claudia – also known as Elena, Susana and Patricia – is being interrogated as we speak."

"And Carlota," I added.

"What?"

"Nothing," I said, as if she hadn't been asked about that unfashionable alias I'd be as well to mention it no more.

"What that woman – whose real name is María José Carrillo Méndez – says is crucial to our defence. At the moment they believe you to have been duped by that unscrupulous lady, due mainly to your mental instability, so if she corroborates what you said we may get a *juicio rápido*."

"A quicky trial? Do they do those?"

"For offences that carry a maximum penalty of less than five years, yes, in certain circumstances. There's a huge backlog of cases, you see, and this is how they're trying to reduce it."

"Fine by me. In and out, eh?"

"Possibly, but there is one condition."

"Go on."

"You must plead guilty."

"What? Me? Guilty? Never! I'm as innocent as the day I was born. She tricked me, that's all."

He smiled thinly. "You must plead guilty to transporting unidentified merchandise from point A to point B."

"Not unidentified, but truffles."

"Unidentified because you didn't *see* the merchandise."

"That's true. Funny that, because I used to take a peek."

"What?"

I gulped behind my hand. "You know, back in England whenever I took anything from point A to point B I'd always like to see what it was."

He frowned. "Have you done this kind of thing before?"

"No, no, I mean, for instance, I once carried a parcel to Kendal for my friend Jeremy, who I guess you'll have already met. It was a long, brown package for a former colleague of his who'd retired to a little cottage in Oxenholme, a village just outside Kendal. I took it on Carmela, my Harley Davidson motorbike, which I later sold, far too cheaply, but never mind. Anyway, I stopped off at a garage on the way there, to fill up, and I couldn't resist peeling back the paper a bit. Can you guess what it was?"

"No."

"A foot pump."

"What?"

"A foot pump, for bicycle tyres, though you can use them on car tyres too if you have the right adapter. I should have guessed what it was by the shape, and the fact that Jeremy had been doing a bit of cycling but had packed it in and gone back to his hiking, but I still couldn't resist looking. I stuck the tape back down after though, so I don't think the old fellow knew I'd looked."

"Is this how you spoke to the policemen yesterday?"

"Yes, more or less."

"Then we have a chance. The female suspect is probably going to get life, as there's a catalogue of crimes attributed to her that would astonish you."

"Don't bet... yes, I bet they would."

"She is, as they say in legal parlance, f*cked, so we just have to hope that she has the common decency not to incriminate you. It would do her no good, after all."

"Honour among thieves, eh?"

"That's not quite what I was thinking, but yes, I suppose so."

I stroked my chin and thought hard. "Listen, er... Benito. Would it help matters if I told you the whole story? You know, in case Claudia turns out to lack that common decency you mentioned."

He grimaced and covered his ears. "No, no, I do not. A lawyer's job is hard enough, without hearing true stories." He shivered and nervously fingered his tie. "I'll go now, but will monitor proceedings. If they question you again, respond in the same way as yesterday, but don't act as if you're mad. Just say whatever enters your head and all will be well."

"OK. Will you not be present?"

"No, I shall be working behind the scenes."

"Did my pals hire you here in Cartagena? You know, a quick shufty at the phonebook till they found a nice name?"

"They did not. I am a friend of Laura's. We met at the Belgian embassy in Madrid some years ago. She was kind enough to put some work my way, so now it's time to return the favour."

"Well I never. Ha, it's not what you know, but who you know, eh?"

"Let's hope this proves to be the case, for your sake." He smoothed his lapels and sniffed sniffily. "I'll have you know that I'm a respected criminal lawyer, the like of whom most delinquents could only dream of hiring, and I've driven down from Madrid at the behest of that fine lady who you are extremely fortunate to know."

"I'll say."

"My name carries much weight, even here."

"I'll bet it does. I'm very grateful, Benito. I'd like to invite you to dinner when I get out, to show my appreciation, seeing as you're not going to charge me."

"*If* you get out. I must go now."

"OK, hasta mañana. Check out the Roman theatre if you get the chance. I hope to see it myself soon."

***

My second interrogation, which took place the following morning, proved to be much shorter than the first. In the same room as the previous day I was privileged to meet Doctor Casillas, a fat man in a creased suit rather than the bow-tied, goatee-bearded shrink I'd expected to see, though he was wearing thick, round specs that magnified his watery blue eyes. Young Jorge was there too, but instead of Isidro he was accompanied by a uniformed officer with a military bearing and lots of stripes and pips, so I assumed he was one of the station's top cops, if not the boss man himself.

"Where's Isidro?" I asked Jorge, who seems a bit nervous in the presence of his superior.

"Sick," he whispered, before looking down and shuffling through some notes.

"Señor Corless, please tell us in your own words what happened on the night of the twenty-fourth of this month," said the doc, twiddling a biro and running his tongue along his upper teeth, first one way and then the other.

"In the early hours of the twenty-fifth, actually," I said with a grin, before beginning to relate the events in the painstaking detail that only those of us with total recall can achieve. I started off at the second-to-last place where I'd taken coffee prior to driving to La Isleta del Moro, and I was about to climb into Bambi about an hour later, both in real time and the time I'd taken to recount that uneventful interlude, when the doctor raised both his hands and pushed his palms forward several times.

"That's enough, don't you think?" he said to the senior cop.

"In view of the testimony of... her, I see no reason to proceed further," he muttered in the doctor's ear, but my razor-sharp hearing caught every word. "And I'm hungry," he whispered, but I heard that too.

He turned to me. "Tomorrow you will be tried," he said in his normal voice.

"A quickie, eh, officer?"

"Take him back to the cell," he said to Jorge, before he and the doc left without another word.

As Jorge appeared to be disinclined to converse I allowed him to lead me back to my cell in silence. After unlocking the door and ushering me inside I saw a nervous smile playing upon his harassed face, so I felt the least I could do was to thank him for the part he had played in securing me a quickie trial.

"You're the luckiest man alive," he replied, before patting the part of his left cheek that was still playing up.

"I'd cut down on the coffee, if I were you," I said, playfully imitating his tick. "Yes, I guess I'm pretty lucky, but I've had a tough time recently, so it's about time I got a break. Say hello to Isidro for me when you see him."

"If I see him," he said, before leaning on the door frame for so long that I thought he might be angling for a tip, so I told him that unfortunately I wasn't in possession of my wallet.

"What?"

"Otherwise I'd have given you a little something. Perhaps you could join us when I take Benito, my lawyer, to dinner."

"Adiós, Chef," he croaked, before shutting and locking the door, so I shrugged and lay down on my bed to peruse the sports pages of the *Revista Oficial del Cuerpo Nacional de Policía*.

***

I awoke the following morning full of optimism, as the sun was shining through the tiny barred window and I could sense that my bowels were going to function correctly for the first time in three days, despite a total absence of brown bread from the police station diet. After a breakfast of orange juice, toast and instant coffee I was inspecting my soiled collar when yet another policeman arrived.

"Come on, you're going to see your lawyer and then to trial," he said brusquely, so I showed him the offending collar.

"I can't possibly appear in court with this collar, young man. I have more shirts in Bambi and would be grateful if you could nip down and get one."

The swarthy chap gave me a lopsided grin, almost a sneer. "No-one'll be looking, now get a move on."

"I know who got out of the bed on the wrong side this morning," I said as I buttoned my shirt.

To my surprise he plugged his ears with his fingers.

"What's up?" I mouthed.

"I've been warned not to listen to you. You're not going to get to *me*," he said, before pushing me out of the door.

"I've a good mind to make a complaint," I said to Benito a few moments later. "I've been manhandled."

"Shut up and sit down."

I snorted and complied.

"Right, Geoff, I've got some good news for you."

"I'm free to go?"

"Not yet, but Claudia, or whatever she's called, not only corroborated your story about meeting her at the hotel and all the rest, but she also strengthened our case by stating that you were clearly not in your right mind during the time she spent with you."

"Well, I was sort of thinking with this." I pointed down at my lap. "As she's a tasty piece, you know."

"When asked directly about your psychological state she laughed out loud and said you had the mental age of an infant. I know this because of my connections. A crummy Cartagena lawyer would not have been privy to this information."

"I shall be eternally grateful to you, Benito. She's wrong, of course, but I don't think I'll contradict her at the trial."

"At the trial you will say nothing. The judge and I have already spoken and we will conclude matters as quickly as possible. Come on, let's get it over with."

To my surprise he led me down the corridor and into a room not much bigger than the one we'd left; about twelve feet by ten, I'd say, with an old table and four chairs.

"Who's that?" I asked Benito, pointing to a greasy-haired, bearded gent of about forty-five, whose tie was askew and his head buried in papers.

"That's the judge."

"You're joking. What about the wig and the red robes?"

The alleged judge looked up wearily from his reading and signalled me to be seated. He then began to speak to Benito at great speed and in such a monotonous voice that I soon lost the thread and began to fidget in my chair, not having changed my underwear since the day before that fateful night. I'd been allowed to shower once, but as I said to the cop who escorted me to the bathroom, what's the point of showering if you have to put on the same crusty boxers? After that and other reveries I heard something tapping on the table, which proved to be the end of a pen.

"Sign here, here and here."

"Is that it?"

"You tell him," the jaded 'judge' said to Benito.

"Due to diminished responsibility you will not be required to serve a prison term. Instead the court sentences you to pay a fine of three thousand euros. Once the payment has been made, you will be free to go. Now sign."

"Ooh, I bet they looked at my rug money to see how much they could squeeze out of me," I said to Benito, as the other chap had already turned away and opened a new file.

"There, there and… there," he said, guiding my hand from page to page.

"Adiós, Agustín," he said to the judge.

"Hasta luego, Benito" the judge replied, before giving me a withering look and showing me his balding pate.

"I'd sort of hoped for something a bit more showy," I said to Benito out in the corridor, but he just nodded and fiddled with his briefcase. "What now then?"

"You'll go back to the cell and they'll sort you out."

I glanced out of an unbarred window into a small courtyard. "Ah, it'll be nice to get out. Can I just say once again how grateful I am for your help, Benito," I said, but on turning my head he was nowhere to be seen.

"Ah, there's nowt as queer as folk," I said with a sigh, before trotting off to complete the formalities.

14

When I emerged from the police station into the sunlight I found Laura and Jeremy waiting for me. In films when people are released after a harrowing courtroom ordeal their loved ones normally whoop for joy and smother them with hugs and kissed, but I saw right away that this wasn't going to occur. Laura did smile briefly on seeing me, but Jeremy's face was stony to say the least.

"That's sorted then. Thanks a lot, guys," I said, the English words tripping off my tongue like long-lost friends.

"That's all right," said Laura, patting my arm.

I held out my hand to Jeremy, and on being forced to shake it he smiled wryly and shook his head.

"You've excelled yourself this time, Geoff."

"I know, that's to say things got a little out of control. I have to get Bambi now. Then we could go and see the Roman theatre."

"I'm going to get off now," said Laura. "Jeremy's going to drive back with you, as I'm going to take the opportunity to visit a friend in Murcia, then drive back tomorrow." She smiled pensively at me. "Or the day after."

I chuckled. "Not a friend like Hugo, I hope?"

She frowned, as I might have known she would. "Benito tells me that the woman's declaration suggests that Hugo disappeared some time ago and is presumed dead. It appears that a man called Axel took over his business and at that point they began to deal in drugs. Axel is now on the run."

"That's a shame – for Hugo, I mean – though I never saw him again after that first meeting," I said with great sincerity, as it was true. "And I really did believe I was going to be transporting truffles, scout's honour."

"Hmm, truffles were also mentioned in her declaration," said Jeremy.

"Anything else?" I asked casually.

"I don't know," he replied, gazing searchingly into my eyes, so I turned to Laura.

"The truth is, I did meet Claudia, as I called her, some time ago, but it was Italian white truffles all the way as far as I was concerned."

"I'm sure it was, Geoff. I'm sure you can all discuss it thoroughly, before I get back," she said, after which she took her leave and went to retrieve her car.

Jeremy and I just stood there for a while, me scratching my nose and him gazing at the police station.

"Roman theatre then, after I get Bambi and change my undies?"

"No, Geoff, we'll set off back right away if you don't mind. June and I are on holiday, after all."

"Oh, of course," I said with empathy, though being retired their lives were one long holiday compared to us grafters. "Let's get back and you can carry on where you left off."

"I wish. Harry isn't a happy man."

"Taken it badly, has he? Probably annoyed at me for fibbing about Hugo, though I swear I never saw him again. I'll explain it to him when we get back, to clear the air."

"The less said the better, I think. You are now a *persona non grata* in his book, so just try to stay out of his way until he cools off."

"Oh well, all's well that ends well," I said some time later as I manoeuvred Bambi out of the city and onto the motorway.

"Has it, though?"

"What?"

"Ended well. What are you going to do now?"

"Hm, well, I haven't got much cash left, so I'll have to put my thinking cap on."

"The hotel cost about four hundred euros for the three of us, by the way," he said, looking straight ahead.

"Nice, was it?"

"Four star, but Laura got us a deal."

"She's certainly a resourceful woman, isn't she?"

"If it weren't for her, and Benito, you might be serving a long prison sentence now."

"Hmm, that's certainly food for thought."

"And it's a minor miracle that the woman Claudia spoke as she did. According to Benito she went out of her way to get you off the hook. Remarkable considering she may be tried for murder, among other things."

"Oh, she won't have killed Hugo, no way. She wasn't the murdering type. No, I bet that Axel fed him to the pigs. He really had some, apparently. Maybe I should appear as a witness at her trial."

"You'll do no such thing, you numbskull," he said, harsh words from him, as he isn't a serial blasphemer like Harry.

"No, maybe not. Still, good old Claudia, eh? And I was *this* far from getting her into the sack."

"Yes, Geoff. Now, since we have time to kill, would you like to discuss your future now, or wait till we get back to Laura's house."

I pictured Harry, June and Jeremy; one scowling, one glowering and the other, Jeremy, just gazing like a teacher at a recalcitrant pupil. "How about now?"

"Right. How much money have you got left?"

"Oh, about five hundred, I think," I said, shaving a bit off, as one does.

"Minus four hundred for the hotel bill, leaves one hundred."

"Er, right, yes, of course," I said, as it was only fair that I should foot the bill, seeing as it had been mostly business and they hadn't even seen the Roman theatre.

"Which means you are effectively skint, *ergo* you must fly back with us a few days from now."

"To England?"

"Where else?"

I focussed on the sewage wagon in front of me and felt my heart sinking in my ribcage. The last thing in the world I wished to do was to go back there, not after becoming reacquainted with my beloved Spain and beginning to make some progress in the world of work. Bambi was still running like a dream, so if I could only think of a way to make some cash – legally, of course – what was to stop me staying on and avoiding yet another English winter? Money, of course, or lack of it, as a few hundred euros wouldn't go far and I doubted that Jeremy, let alone Harry, would lend me any, given my recent debacle. Maybe my best bet would be to accept the offer of a plane ticket home, spend the winter working and return to Spain in the spring, having stored Bambi somewhere in the meantime.

"The first thing you'll have to do when you get back is find somewhere to live," said Jeremy.

"Oh, I hadn't thought of that. It could be a bit tricky without a penny to my name. I don't suppose I could stay at yours for a while, could I?" I said, with great cunningness, as I knew that June would loathe having me under her rather large feet, so the prospect might enable me to wheedle a small loan out of them in order to stay in Spain, as she undoubtedly held the purse strings in that household, with a grip of iron.

"I've been giving it some thought."

Uh-oh, I thought. "Oh, yes?" I said.

"Yes, as soon as we get back you'll have to speak to Social Services in Kendal. As you're destitute they'll be obliged to provide you with a flat, and you'll get the dole, of course. I'm sure you'll soon find a job and get back on your feet, at which point you'll be able to pay back any money we've lent you."

"Oh, it's not so easy to get a council flat nowadays, Jeremy. There's a heck of a waiting list, I believe."

"June was looking into that online. As you're over fifty you'll be higher up the list than younger folk. In fact, only next year you'll turn fifty-five, so they ought to take pity on you."

I chuckled. "You're mistaken there, Jeremy. It'll be a long time before I turn fifty-five."

I saw a compassionate smile out of the corner of my eye. "I don't think you realise how old you are, Geoff."

"Of course I do. I'm fifty-two."

"No, that was last year. I know your age has been a moot point since you turned fifty, but you'll be fifty-four in November, *ergo* you'll be fifty-five next year."

"I wish you wouldn't say that."

"But it's undeniable."

"No, I mean *ergo*. You sound like a teacher."

"Ha, yes, and speaking of teaching, June might be able to line up a few Spanish classes for you while you're staying at our house."

"Ha, as if I needed them!"

"No, I mean teaching Spanish, to a couple of local kids. That way you could earn a bit of cash to pay your board until you get your flat. June's thought it all through you see, as she's as concerned for your welfare as I am."

The prospect of teaching the language of Cervantes to a pair of Lancastrian whippersnappers appealed to me even less than being under June's reproving gaze for any length of time, so I turned my attention to the sewage truck and racked my brains for a way to raise some cash. My designer clothes might fetch a few bob, but I'd need those to cut a dash in whatever venture I ventured into, so it was a dejected Geoff Corless who motored those final sinuous miles up the hill to Canillas.

My mood scarcely improved on arrival, as despite greeting Harry and June in as upbeat a manner as I could muster, my reception was decidedly frosty. Harry just grunted and left the room, while June gazed at me as if I were something the dog, rather than her husband, had brought in. When she later loosened up over a cup of tea things got worse rather than better, as she lost no time in outlining her plans for me. These were much as Jeremy had described, except that she intended to oversee my every step towards a stable, civilised life.

"You're not getting any younger, Geoff, so it's too late for you to have any sort of career, but I'm sure we'll still be able to find you a half-decent job, as you can't have burnt *all* your bridges," she said, as if she were talking to one of the thousands of sprogs who had passed through her uncompromising hands.

"Yes, June."

"And I've sent an email to Social Services in Kendal asking if you'd be eligible for one of those little flats for older people and… other people. Supported living, I think they call those schemes. If you get an interview you'll have to pretend to be a bit helpless and sort of simple, then they might let you in."

"Shouldn't be difficult," said Harry from the kitchen, the first words he'd address to me, or about me, since I'd arrived two hours earlier.

"Ha, June, the problem is that I look much younger than my chronological age. They'd take one look at me and tell me to come back in twenty years."

"Deluded pillock," said Harry, still not showing his face.

As I felt it wasn't the time to boast about my conquest of Alina, I just smiled enigmatically and sipped my tea.

"Once you're working again you can find another place to live," Jeremy said soothingly. "Hmm, what'll we do with Bambi?"

"Scrap it," said June.

"I could drive her back," I said, feeling the first real flush of optimism since realising that I wouldn't be spending my remaining sexually active years in jail. "Yes, then I could live in her, so I wouldn't be wasting money on rent."

"You'd freeze to death, and besides, you can't afford to take her back," said Jeremy.

I chose that moment to make my heartfelt plea for freedom. "Look, I'd like to stay in Spain, so if you could, er… lend me a bit of cash, which I'll pay back asap, I could find a job and make a go of it here." I looked around to see only gestapo-like faces. "I'd even go to work in one of those infernal greenhouses near the coast. Anything rather than going home and pretending to be an aging halfwit."

Harry popped his head around the door. "That's just…" he began, but Jeremy shushed him.

"Geoff, remember that you've now got a criminal record in Spain. It'd be practically impossible to get a job. Do the sensible thing and come back with us."

"I'll take Bambi off your hands," said Harry, finally stepping into the room.

"What?"

"Laura knows of an old garage we can use. I'll buy her off you, store her for the winter, then maybe we'll take a trip in her next year."

I smiled. "What, the three of us again?"

Harry smiled back. "No, Laura and me."

"How much then?"

"Two hundred euros."

"But she cost me over three thousand quid!"

"That was then and this is now. Her MOT will run out soon, so I'll have to get her re-registered here, which costs money. Plus you managed to knacker her rear end. Two hundred, take it or leave it."

"He'll take it," said my self-appointed social worker.

"Whoa," I said, remembering Harry's fondness for haggling. "I'll take a thousand, not a penny less."

"Two hundred."

"Nine-fifty."

"Two hundred."

"Nine hundred."

"Two hundred."

"Aw, you're not playing the game!"

Harry shrugged his gross shoulders and left the room. I stared at the floor until I felt Jeremy's hand on my back.

"Take it, Geoff. Look, never mind about paying us board for now. You can keep the two hundred for beer money, then we'll be able to go down the pub from time to time."

"I don't think–" June began.

"Shush, dear. What do you say, eh?"

I slumped onto the sofa and held my head in my hands. Is this what I'd been reduced to? After earning big bucks all summer long and bedding or nearly bedding several stunners, here I was, being patronised by Jeremy, humiliated by Harry and practically sectioned by June. On looking up to see banknotes between Harry's fat fingers, I snatched them away, thus completing my capitulation.

"Let's have a drink," said the great greedy lump, and after a beer or three the tension began to ease and we were chatting away like normal folk. As I saw that the sun was about to set I said that I'd better go and get my stuff from Bambi.

"Bring the documents while you're at it," said Harry with a kindly gaze, which I found more galling than his previous leers, sneers and smirks.

Out on the street I breathed in the cool evening air and looked down toward the coast. As the sky began to redden, so did my eyes, I think, as the end of my summer odyssey caused me great sadness, not to mention the ordeal which awaited me back in the frozen north. I wrenched open the back door and began to collect the clothes that the police had strewn around during their search. As I stuffed them into a black plastic bag – for they all needed washing, some more than others – I perceived that one pair of dirty socks weighed more than the others, and upon unrolling the fetid things a hard object fell to the floor.

"It's Claudia's watch," I said aloud, before hearing her sweet voice again. *'I mean, it cost me over three thousand euros,'* she'd said back at the Iberostar Hotel on the eve of the night of passion that wasn't to be, and, alas, never would, as by the time she got out I really would be a middle-aged man. I kissed the watch and slipped it into my pocket, before closing the door, climbing into the cab, starting her up and easing my faithful camper van down the narrow street.

"There'll be time enough for thinking tomorrow," I murmured as I steered her onto the open road.

Printed in Poland
by Amazon Fulfillment
Poland Sp. z o.o., Wrocław